Call of the
LOON

Photography © 1995: Robert W. Baldwin: 16, 17, 32, 34-35, 39, 42, 45, 54, 58-59, 60, 63, 74-75, 76, 80, 81, 86-87, 95, 96-97, 102-103, 112, 119, 120, 130, 138, 140, Back cover. Dembinsky Photo Associates: 2-3, 14-15, 23, 26-27, 41, 43, 46, 51, 66-67, 106-107, 110-111, 118, 121-122, 142-143. DRK Photo: W. Lankinen: 21, 93, 115; S. Nielsen: 68-69, 133. The Wildlife Collection: 79, 127. Bill Kinney: Front cover, 1, 18-19, 22, 24, 36-37, 53, 98-99. Bruce Coleman, Inc.: 9, 83. Gregory M. Nelson: 13, 33, 38, 52, 56-57, 72-73, 100-101, 105, 137. Dominique Braud: 49, 90-91. Stephen Kirkpatrick: 10-11, 88-89, 117. Art Wolfe: 28. Alaska Stock Images: 31.

NorthWord Press, Inc.
P.O. Box 1360
Minocqua, WI 54548

Cover design by Russell S. Kuepper
Book design by Lisa Moore

Library of Congress Cataloging-in-Publication Data
Strong, Paul I.V.
     Call of the Loon/ by Paul Strong.
        p.   cm. – (Camp and cottage series)
     Includes bibliographical references (p.   ).
     ISBN 1-55971-458-1
     1. Loons. I. Title. II. Series : Camp & cottage series.
QL696.G33S77   1995
598. 4'2–dc20   94-41780

Printed in the Hong Kong

For a free catalog describing NorthWord's line of nature books and gift items, call toll free 1-800-336-5666

Call of the
LOON

by Paul Strong

NorthWord
PRESS, INC.

Minocqua, Wisconsin

DEDICATION

To my parents, Charles and Mary Strong, who raised me on a loon lake in Maine, taught me the names of the plants and animals, instilled in me a respect for nature and a sense of wonder, and gave me many wonderful outdoor experiences. Without you, none of this would have been possible.

ACKNOWLEDGMENTS

I am fortunate to have met many wonderful people who know about and are interested in loons. Although I have acquired much knowledge about loons through my own research, much more has come from other scientists and people who watch loons. There are far too many people to be named who have contributed to my picture of loons and the fascinating relationship between loons and people. As an apology and a disclaimer, people not mentioned here are not unimportant, only part of a large unnamed group to whom I owe a great deal.

Some people deserve special mention. Barbara Harold was a wonderful and patient editor. Tom Klein gave me my first job and an opportunity to use what I knew about loons at the time to good purpose. Members of the North American Loon Fund's Board of Trustees and of the LoonWatch Advisory Council were sources of information and inspiration. Ed Miller shared his exciting research results, and our late night discussions stimulated new thinking about loon society. Jimmy Pichner taught me about the early life of loon chicks and plumage changes. I have always looked forward to Jeff Wilson's questions and ideas about loons—they made me rethink what seemed obvious and often wasn't. Dave Evers brought me up to date on the results of his banding research. The late Laurence Alexander shared his many ideas about the winter ecology of loons. Terry Daulton kept me in the loop of loon happenings after I completed my tenure as LoonWatch Coordinator.

Literally hundreds of amateur loon watchers have added to my knowledge base and perspective. You all are important, but especially Bill and Linda Bein and the late Jack Dudley.

I worked with six great guys during three magical summers when I was conducting loon studies in northern Maine. I would have perished without them and they offered the logistical, spiritual, and intellectual support I needed. Thanks to Rob Burke, Fred Dibello, Pat Jodice, Dennis Kingman, Jr., Rick Souza, and Chuck Terry.

My graduate school advisor, John Bissonette, was my professional mentor and is a friend. Thanks for all of those valuable lessons, John.

Jeff Fair continues to be a friend, critic, and kindred spirit. Jeff's knowledge of and enthusiasm for loons and their conservation inspire me.

Susan, thank you for everything, for editing my writing, suggesting improvements, sharing your views, and mostly, for keeping your heart close to mine.

PREFACE

The loon swims in the margins of our ancestral memory much as it seems to float on the mist of a northern lake. Its silhouette is unmistakable, its manner stoic. It links us to a past we do not understand, a seemingly ancient bird in a modern world. Wildness is its signature, reminding us of a time and place when people shared the world more equitably with their animal brethren.

We hunger to know everything about loons. We think it is right in front of us, on our lakes. The drama of the loon's life unfolds every summer day on this small stage. Yet much of the play is partially acted out in places we do not see, in a language we cannot interpret, with motions for which we have no analogue, and by actors seemingly aloof to their audience.

Native peoples thought the loon strong and brave. Our great nature writers attribute nobility to it. Yet the loon is far more complex. The efforts of researchers, dedicated conservationists, and casual observers have added pieces to the puzzle that is the loon, but we can misinterpret these data with a bias caused by the loon's symbolic stature.

Somewhere between the shores of symbolism and the hard scientific facts, swims the true nature of the loon. For better or worse, our perception of loons is limited not only by what we are able to see, but how we are able to see it.

As a student of loons for more than a decade, I have observed loons as an intensely focused scientist and as a seeker of spiritual experiences. I have devotedly cataloged loon behavior and subjected it to rigorous statistical manipulations. And, in the presence of loons, I have felt the manifestation of some otherworldly force, the essence that binds all living things. I have allowed myself to experience these moments in ways that result in no new data, but forever etch a new feeling in my memory.

Our ability to characterize loons is still incomplete, but our need to do so is so strong that we give the loon attributes it may or may not have. It is with a mix of excitement and disappointment that we discover something new that shatters the image we have developed.

I have always tried to keep the loon's picture limited, leaving room for new knowledge and a view from a different perspective. Now, I commit to paper what I and many others have learned about this magnificent work of Nature so that you can form your own image of the loon. Keep your mind open to the possibilities . . .

What's in a Name

The English-speaking people of North America know the five living species of the genus *Gavia* as loons, a name derived from a Scandinavian word meaning clumsy for the way loons move around on land. The British have a much more apt name for these superbly adapted aquatic birds. They call them divers. Our common loon, a bird whose name lacks panache, is known as the "great northern diver," a much more romantic and evocative term to my way of thinking.

Native peoples of North America knew the loon as an important part of

their environment. Their cultures included the loon in creation stories and a number of other legends, some of which have been passed down and are still alive today. Various tribes had different names for loons. Several Inuit tribes had names that were similar to the word *Too-lik*. The Ojibway, or Chippewas, who occupied much of the Upper Midwest where common loons were abundant, knew the loon as *mahng* which translates roughly to "brave-hearted one." Some of my ancestors, in tribes occupying New England and the Maritime Provinces of Canada, called loons *hukweem* or *kwee-moo*.

Loons did not hold any special cultural significance with early European settlers of North America, but in the mid-1970s, as people all over the world started to become aware of the importance of the environment, the loon gained status as a symbol of wild, unspoiled things. Over the last twenty years, the common loon has achieved almost cult status. It is *the* symbol of northern lakes. People respond to their love of loons by putting the bird's picture on everything from tee shirts to jewelry to furniture. Although most people are not blind fanatics about loons, anyone who has been in a room full of people listening to a talk about loons can feel the intensity of their interest.

CHAPTER 1

Classification

Family Ties

Imagine the family tree of all birds as a living tree. The tree is very tall with many large and small branches and thousands of twigs. Some of the branches have no living twigs while others have a mix of living and dead. Each twig represents a different species of bird and collectively, the twigs are all of the species of birds that have ever lived. Twigs on the same branchlet are closely related species while those on separate branches are related only distantly. The length of the branch sections represents time, long branches without many forks indicate a long period of time without much evolution of new species. Short

23

branch sections with many forks indicate more rapid development of new species.

On this family tree of birds, there is a branch forking off the main trunk fairly close to the ground. The branch divides and then divides again. At the end of one branchlet are five living twigs, the five species of loons known to exist today. A small number of dead twigs are on other nearby branchlets—fairly recent (two to six million years ago) but now extinct species of loons.

Unlike many of the other branches on the tree, the one with loons at the end has few forks and twigs and the branch sections are long. To find the nearest living relatives of loons one must go back along a branch 40 to 50 million years and then follow a new branch to a group of living twigs representing penguins and species of birds known as tube-nosed swimmers, which include petrels and albatrosses.

The majority of birds that exist today are twigs at the ends of more divided branches near the top of our "tree." The loons, while not primitive birds, are more closely tied to their ancestral stock.

Over the past few decades, there has been considerable debate about the evolutionary classification of loons. Some would tie them closely to grebes, another bird well suited to swimming and diving, but recent studies have demonstrated that grebes and loons are not closely related even though they have adapted to aquatic life in many of the same ways.

One line of thinking has modern-day loons evolving directly from some ancient forms of aquatic birds that swam on the oceans and inland seas. Known as *Hesperornis*, these birds were large fish-eaters, which superficially resembled loons. However, they were much larger and had several key differences which have convinced most scientists that there is no link between them and loons. Instead, they are considered evolutionary dead ends with no modern species having evolved from them.

The classification of the five species of loons recognized today and the relationships between them have changed over time as better techniques for studying relationships have been developed. The same DNA-matching technique used to determine that humans and chimpanzees share almost all of the same DNA has been used on three of the five species of loons. The results indicate that the DNA of the three species are almost indistinguishable and that the species must therefore be very closely related.

Of the five loons, the red-throated seems to be the most different. Much smaller than the others, it has strikingly different plumage, specifically lacking the iridescent head feathers of the breeding plumage and the large white

Arctic loon

spots on the back feathers. It has the largest wings for its body size and is the only loon species that can take off directly from land.

The Pacific and Arctic loons are most closely related to each other and are more closely related to the common and yellow-throated than to the red-throated. Until 1985, the two were considered varieties, or subspecies, of the same species. Then, the American Ornithologist's Union decided that there was enough evidence to list them as separate species. Although they are difficult to tell apart, they are geographically separated over most of their range, the Arctic occurring primarily in Europe and Asia and the Pacific in North America.

Pacific and Arctic loons are smaller than common loons, weighing an average of six to eight pounds. During the breeding season, their heads are adorned with beautiful silvery gray feathers. They have a wide black patch on the front of their neck with white stripes on the sides. Although slightly different from those of the common loon, the back and wing feathers have the classic combination of large and small white spots on a black background.

Common and Pacific loons overlap in their breeding ranges, particularly in Alaska. This has occasionally led to mixed breeding pairs. While conducting environmental studies for oil companies in Alaska, Ian Robertson and Mark Fraker found a family of loons comprised of one adult common loon, one adult Pacific loon, and their two young. There was no verification of the parents of the young, but it seems most likely that they were the products of the two adults. That a hybrid loon might survive to adulthood is suggested by observations made in Scotland in 1970 by E. N. Hunter and R. H. Dennis. They watched and obtained film of a loon that appeared to be an adult common-Arctic loon hybrid based on plumage patterns.

The common loon is most closely related to the somewhat larger, but strikingly similar, yellow-billed loon. The two appear almost identical in their breeding plumage with the exception of bill color. The best scientific speculation is that the two species came about during one of the glacial periods in the last fifty thousand years.

We know that not all areas in Canada and Alaska were covered by ice even when the glaciers were creeping into the northern tier of the United States. One area in central Alaska stayed ice-free, and common loons that had been breeding there before glaciation continued to use that area while most of the continental loons had to use areas far to the south. The northern loons may have had a slightly larger body size as an adaptation to colder temperatures as many animals do. The origin of the yellow bill is unknown, but it is likely a genetic trait that arose by chance and persisted in the small population that was isolated by the glaciers. When the glaciers receded, the common loons that had been pushed to the south expanded their range to the north and took advantage of newly created lakes for breeding areas. The yellow-billed loons apparently stayed isolated enough to limit hybridization and became different enough for us to classify them as a distinct species.

CHAPTER 2

Form and Function

A Feathered Fish

Birds are gloriously variable. Over the course of millions of years, they have diverged in body shape and have exploited many ecological niches. Some species of closely related birds have very different shapes such as the severely endangered Hawaiian honeycreepers whose bill shapes and lengths reflect the variable foods they use. Other closely related species like the loons are far less variable with very little difference among the species in either their shape or way of life.

Although loons superficially resemble some early and now extinct forms of birds, over the millennia,

they have evolved highly specialized characteristics that help them master their watery milieu. Only penguins show greater specialization for aquatic life and in doing so have given up the ability to fly.

Unlike penguins, evolution has not crafted loons as flightless birds. Instead, loons are precariously balanced on the razor's edge between increased specialization for swimming and diving and retention of the ability to fly. It is flight that allows loons to exploit northern lakes full of fish. Without it, loons might be oceanic birds nesting on beaches protected from wave and tidal action. In a way, it is surprising that some populations of loons are not ocean nesters. Certainly, the tides present a problem in nest placement and incubation duties, but it seems plausible that loons could waddle far enough ashore to place their nests safely and could adjust behaviorally in their incubation patterns to deal with long periods of being high and dry.

We know of only one circumstance in North America of loons nesting along the ocean coast. In the

Summer 1990 issue of the Maine Audubon Society's newsletter, *The Loon News*, there was a report of a confirmed ocean nest of a common loon in Hancock County which is about halfway up the coast of Maine. The nest was first seen in 1989 when observers watched an adult loon climb up the rocky shoreline to a nest. Later on, the observers discovered eggshell fragments in the nest, but they could not ascertain whether the pair had successfully hatched young. In 1990, the nest was used again, but it failed, apparently to predation by birds (likely gulls, which

are abundant along the Maine coast).

If one thinks about loons' physical adaptations in reference to their ability to move around in and on water, land, and the air, it is clear that evolutionary forces have directed loons primarily toward proficiency at swimming and diving while leaving them limited abilities to walk and moderate competency to fly. And so, loons are sometimes known as "feathered fish" for they sometimes seem more finny than feathery.

Perhaps the most obvious features of loons for swimming and diving are

their streamlined body shape and the position of their legs. Underwater, a loon's body seems to flatten from the top and bottom and to cut through the water like a saucer. The massive muscles in the upper leg that provide the powerful propulsion are part of the loon's torso to reduce drag in the water. The rear-positioned legs allow for maximum efficiency. Large webbed feet push literally gallons of water with every few strokes.

During dives, a loon holds its head and neck directly in front of its body unless it is about to strike at a fish it is pursuing. Even the connection of the spinal cord to the head helps with streamlining. The opening in the skull is more directly behind the head instead of below it, which allows the head to be held in front of the neck comfortably.

Loons possess special flaps in the nostrils and at the back of the throat that close when they are swimming. In that way, they can swim with a fish grasped in their bill without ingesting a lot of water.

Most birds have a complex network of air sacs, which are extensions of their lungs, that extend into various chambers of their bodies including bones. Loons have air sacs, but they are much reduced compared to other kinds of birds. In 1952, H. T. Gier, a zoologist at the then Kansas State College, investigated the air sacs of loons by injecting heated paraffin into the lungs and air sacs of a dead loon and then dissecting the specimen. He found that loons have among the simplest air sacs of any kind of bird and that they do not penetrate into any bone. In fact, in most birds, bones are either hollow or have air spaces in them so that overall body weight is reduced and flight is easier. Loons, on the other hand, have solid bones, which help them achieve greater weight to be more proficient at diving.

Adult common loons in the summer typically weigh between eight and fourteen pounds. There is a great deal of variation throughout the world as well as in any one area. In general, loons in the Midwest are the smallest while those along the northeast and northwest coasts of North America are the largest. Their density (the ratio between weight and body size) is nearly that of water which makes them barely buoyant and is just one more way that loons are adapted to a diving lifestyle. Loons can sink like a submarine just by pressing their feathers closely to their body expelling the air trapped between feathers and by exhaling air from their lungs.

While rear-positioned legs are wonderful outboard motors, they are

less than ideal for moving about on land. Adult loons are able to hold their body off the ground, but when they walk, they shuffle along clumsily with their breast dragging. Young chicks walk much more competently because they don't have the same body shape as adults and can balance over their legs easier. Loons are capable of moving quickly on land when they are frightened. At these times, they run while rowing (propelling) with their wings.

Loons rarely come to land other than to sit on the nest, but occasionally one takes a stroll for unknown reasons. Nature writer Sigurd F. Olson described an experience he had with a loon on land in his book, *Listening Point*. He was carrying his canoe on his back as he portaged between two lakes in northern Minnesota when he came upon a loon using the same portage trail. Upon seeing the strange two-legged creature with the long head, the loon gave a loud scream and half ran, half flew down the trail to the lake!

Loon chicks have been seen crossing roads between lakes in northern Wisconsin and crossing levees between pools on the Seney National Wildlife Refuge in Michigan's eastern Upper Peninsula. Their parents apparently fly from one lake to another and call to the chicks who then cross roads or other narrow necks of land between nearby lakes. Although I have never witnessed this behavior, I am sure it happened on my study area in northern Maine one year.

While studying loons during the nesting season, I found a loon chick with its parents on a part of the lake where I was sure no nest had been. Later, I discovered a nest and eggshells on a pond that was just a hundred or so feet from the lake's edge. During years of high water, the land separating the two water bodies was probably covered, but that year there was a maze of driftwood that the chick must have negotiated over and around to get from the nesting pond to the lake.

The running and wing flapping adult loons employ in terror on land is the same they use to lift their heavy bodies off the water to attain flight. To become airborne, loons must take advantage of wind direction and use a runway that sometimes approaches several hundred yards. They start by swimming to the windward side of the lake and begin rowing with their wings. As their body begins to lift off the water breaking the surface tension, which is the force that holds objects to water, they add running. Their wings begin to flap more than row and one can hear the wings ticking the water and their feet splashing in perfect rhythm until they are free of the water and in flight.

The sound of a loon taking off has always attracted me. I heard it often over the course of my three-year

research project and loved it best in the quiet of early morning when the lake was calm and flat as a mirror. It is a delightful sound, and it came back to me in unusual circumstances one summer. I was participating in a Loon Festival in Maine and helping to judge a loon calling contest. The young and old contestants were producing an amusing variety of loon calls. During the adult division, a man asked the crowd and judges to close their eyes and to imagine that they were on a northern lake in the dawn stillness. Like everyone else, I thought he was just trying to set the mood for a haunting wail. Instead, after the crowd had achieved total silence, he began to beat his hands against his chest, first slowly, then more and more rapidly until he stopped and uttered a series of "whooshes." For those of us who had seen and heard a loon taking off in just such a setting, the effect was perfect. The man didn't win the contest, but he got my vote.

Once a loon is airborne, it flies amazingly fast, but not entirely by choice. The length and width of a loon's wing is small for its body size and creates high "wing-loading" compared to other kinds of birds. In order to stay aloft, loons flap their wings at approximately 275 beats per minute, which propels them at speeds upwards of sixty miles per hour. Loons are not able to slow down much, however, unless they are coming in to land. They are not particularly maneuverable and typically fly in straight lines or in wide sweeping arcs. A friend of mine who has studied loons for years has said that loons are the only bird whose average flight speed is 60, but who stall out at 59.

Estimates of flight speed of loons have been done in several ways. Two of the more curious reported in the scientific literature come from a doctor flying his private plane and from a man driving a car. In 1953, Dr. James Pittman was flying his Piper Cub J-3 airplane near Charlotte, North Carolina, when he spotted a loon flying ahead of him. He altered his course and followed the loon for several minutes to check its air speed. Despite accelerating to full throttle of 90 miles per hour, the loon slowly pulled away.

In 1950, F. W. Preston was driving along the St. Lawrence River northeast of Montreal, Canada, and spotted a loon flying low over the river. From the riverside road, he was able to catch up to the loon and keep it in sight as he paced it. The loon's calculated air speed was approximately 62 miles per hour.

"This is Black and White Airlines carrier 101 calling air traffic controller on Round Lake. I'm approaching from the

northeast at 70 miles per hour and the runway is in sight. Do I have clearance to land?"

"Carrier 101. This is ground control. Continue your approach. Other carriers are clearing the runway. Check your flaps and landing gear. Be advised that the runway is choppy and that there are gusting crosswinds."

"Roger, ground control. I am beginning my descent. My touchdown time will be in approximately 30 seconds."

A loon coming in for a landing makes the transition from air to water look like a tenuous affair. While still a hundred feet or so above the lake, it stops flapping and raises its wings in a shallow "V." It sways from side to side and approaches the water at a shallow angle. Touchdown is made on the heavily muscled breast, and the webbed feet are dragged behind to brake the momentum.

Most loons are expert at landing, but they go through a learning period as youngsters and even years of practice can't counteract difficult conditions. I recall watching loons on Millinocket Lake one windy August day when the lake was furious with whitecaps and rollers. Most loons on the lake were floating out the storm with their heads tucked under their wings. I heard the call of a loon in flight and through my binoculars saw an adult loon coming in for a landing. It attempted to land between the waves and appeared to have pulled it off successfully when a large wave crashed over and sent it rolling. The loon called in alarm and dove. When it surfaced, the loon looked around nervously, and I imagined that it was sheepishly hoping that no other loons had witnessed its muffed landing.

Not only do loons have to move about on land, water, and air, they also must deal with different kinds of water. Loons spend at least half of their lives on saltwater and have to rid excess salt from their bodies while they are there. Loons aren't the only birds with this challenge, but their adaptation to saltwater is not the same as all others. Loons have a set of glands just above their eyes which become active when they are on the ocean. Excess salt in the blood is removed by the glands and excreted from the body in a concentrated liquid that comes out of the glands and runs down the bill.

As fish-eaters, loons ingest scales, bones, and spines. They do not have any special adaptations for this, like owls and birds of prey which regurgitate bones and fur in dry pellets. Instead, loons have a heavily muscled gizzard full of pebbles, which grinds even the toughest material and allows it to pass through the digestive system. I wondered just how large and tough a loon's gizzard was until I found a recently dead loon on a lakeshore just outside of Bangor, Maine. I was

amazed to find that the gizzard was difficult to cut with my jackknife. Inside were a dozen or so small rocks that had been worn smooth by all of the grinding. We suspect that loons may actually choose smooth rocks over uneven ones for this task because they seem especially attracted to lead fishing sinkers. Every year, dozens of loons are found dead, apparent victims of lead poisoning from them.

Trying to explain how loons' adaptations are really a series of trade-offs has always been a challenge to me. Several years ago, I spent many of my days and nights giving presentations about loons. Often, I would be asked to talk to schoolchildren.

It was in a third grade classroom in a school in Illinois that I was taught a lesson about loons by a particularly inquisitive and perceptive nine-year-old. He wanted to know why loons weren't better at flying, and I fumbled my way through and around the answer.

He then said, "Oh, you mean that in Nature you can't be good at everything. If you're a good swimmer and diver, you might not be able to fly so well or walk great. Like me at school. My teacher tells me that I'm good at math and reading, but that my spelling is pretty bad."

"Right," I said.

Leave it to a third grader to figure it out best.

A Most Regal Finery

When we conjure up an image of a loon in our minds, most of us see the well known black and white plumage adult loons wear when they are on their northern breeding lakes. Surely, Mother Nature did her best work in designing a most elegant pattern out of only two colors. The pattern is truly striking. Etched into a very basic "black above, white below" pattern seen on seabirds like auks, murres, and razorbills are a white necklace, a chin strap, fine black and white lines across the shoulders, and large and small white spots on the black back and the top side of the wings.

We are not the first people to be impressed by the loon's plumage. Native Americans knew the loon well, sometimes using it for food as did the Cree in northern Quebec, and other times for medicine pouches as did a number of tribes in the interior of Alaska. Loons were often used in creation stories. The legend of how the loon got its necklace is told in a variety of forms across Canada and the northern United States, but the basic premise is the same. The loon, then in more drab plumage than we know it today, helps a blind man restore his sight by diving repeatedly with the man on his back. In return, the man makes an amulet of shells which he throws to the loon. When the necklace lands around the bird's neck, some of the shells break off and become the spots on its back.

Like many species of birds, loons have two outfits in their wardrobe, one worn during the breeding season and called alternate or nuptial plumage, and another worn during winter and called basic plumage. Loons wear their nuptial plumage from about March to October. When we first see them on the breeding grounds in the spring, they have just molted their basic winter plumage and acquired new nuptial feathers. By the time fall migration begins in September, the first stages of the molt into the winter plumage has begun. As loons wing their way south, we sometimes see loons that appear to be growing white moustaches and goatees because the first feathers to be molted are those on the face around the bill.

Fall brings on a complete molt of the body feathers. Loons in winter have dark feathers on their backs, the top of their heads, and back of their necks. The belly, front of the neck, and chin area are white. Body feathers are molted twice annually, but flight feathers on the wings are replaced only once each year. In January, loons drop all of their flight feathers at one time and grow them back over the course of the next two months. This leaves them flightless on the ocean where there are no pressing reasons to fly anyway. When they start spring migration,

their flight feathers are new and strong. Upon completing fall migration some seven or eight months later these same feathers are badly worn and tattered.

We still aren't absolutely sure how old loons are when they first acquire the finery of their breeding plumage, but all evidence suggests that they are about four years old. Loon chicks wear patterns similar to those of adults in the winter, but they molt later in the spring and get the same drab plumage back again. Young loons can be differentiated from adults even in the winter plumage because the outer edges of their back feathers are light, giving their back a scalloped appearance. In the summer, I have seen loons that looked like a dirty version of adults and suspected that they were three-year-old birds one season away from acquiring full breeding colors.

The breakthrough in understanding the pattern of loon feather changes came from the Minnesota Zoo where Jimmy Pichner and his colleagues attempted to hatch and raise loon chicks from eggs laid in the wild. One of their loons lived four years and they carefully recorded the molts the bird went through. In the bird's third spring, it grew feathers with black and white spots and had a faintly outlined necklace. The next year, it had most of the feathers seen on adults. Although it can be argued that a zoo environment threw off the molt pattern, it seems more likely

that the molts represent what happens in the wild and that loons start to get adult breeding plumage at three years old and get full adult plumage at four years. Dave Evers' banding studies of adults and chicks support what Jimmy Pichner saw. Three-year-old loons are found on the breeding grounds, and their plumage is a "dirty" version of the adult type, a number of brown feathers contributing to the "dirty" appearance.

CHAPTER 3

Behavior and Society

The Daily Routine

No matter where they are or what time of year it is, loons perform a number of activities on a daily basis. Like people, they clean themselves, rest, and find things to eat.

Feathers are extremely specialized structures and require a great deal of care. Every day, loons spend hours keeping their feathers clean and straightened. Some ritualistic routines can be enjoyable to watch.

Adults engage in preening several times a day. During a preening session, they use their bills to put oil or water on their feathers. Birds possess an oil gland at the base of their tail.

Squeezing the gland with the bill caus-es oil to be released. When feathers are passed through the bill, they get a coat-ing of oil which makes them more water repellent. This is particularly important for water birds. Oil is not used in every preening session by loons. Sometimes, loons wet their bills in the water before preening.

Back and wing feathers are preened from a normal sitting posture on the water by twisting the head and neck backward. When attention is turned to breast feathers, the head is tucked down in front. Belly feathers are reached by turning on the side,

sometimes almost over on the back. This position is called a rolling preen, and the flash of the white belly is obvious to an observer. Preening the head and neck feathers requires a bit of creativity because loons groom only themselves. Oil is taken from the oil gland and spread on the back feathers. Then, the head and neck are stretched straight back and rubbed vigorously.

Another way loons maintain their feathers is to shake them periodically and to bathe. The head and neck are shaken after a dive to rid them of water. The tail is shaken in a similar fashion. Loons often perform what we call a wing flap to shake out water and straighten the feathers. Usually, a loon faces into the wind, raises its body out of the water, and flaps both wings several times before settling back into the sitting position. Some people have thought this might be a signal to other loons, but it appears to have no communication purpose.

Occasionally, loons roll on their sides or backs and shake their entire body while flapping their wings. This is how they take baths. I remember seeing this for the first time during my research in northern Maine. My partner and I were convinced after watching such behavior for five minutes that the loon had become entangled in fishing line. We approached the loon in the canoe only to find that it was just fine and that we had interrupted its bath.

Over the course of a decade, hundreds of loon lovers have asked me why loons shake their feet above the water. Like the wing flap, they think it may be a signal to other loons. However, the "foot waggle" as it is known is simply a comfort movement.

From time to time, a loon will raise one leg out of the water, stretch it, and shake it several times. If one watches closely, after shaking, the foot is placed under the wing. I suspect this is a way for loons to reduce heat loss to the water. Loons need to maintain a body temperature above 100 degrees in water that may never get warmer than 65 or 70 degrees even on the hottest days.

The foot waggle is used to an advantage by researchers who want to be able to identify individual loons. Back in the 1980s, I made colored plastic leg bands by heating up strips of thick plastic just enough to make them pliable and wrapping them around a wooden dowel that had been sanded down to the size and shape of a loon's leg. Each plastic strip was wrapped around the dowel several times so that each band could be sized to fit the individual loon and would stay on. Early banding efforts used these bands, but today, researchers like Dave Evers and Mike Meyer are using a new and improved version and are putting different color combinations of these bands on loons they capture and release. When a loon performs a foot waggle, they can see the bands and tell which bird it is.

Loons sleep during the day and at night although we don't know how long an average nap is or how many hours in a day they spend resting. Almost all sleep is done on the water, although sick loons may come to shore to rest, and I have seen loons that appear to be nodding off as they sit on their nests.

Typical sleeping posture is the head tucked over the back with the bill buried in the wing feathers. Loon chicks sleep with their heads held to the side. Often, one of the feet will be tucked up under a wing while the other foot paddles slowly to keep the loon in place.

Like most animals, loons spend much of their time finding food. Despite the decades of loon research and the scores of people who have watched loons carefully, we know relatively little about what loons eat. The biggest problem is that loons catch their prey underwater and eat all but the largest things there. Only rarely do we see adults bring a fish to the surface before swallowing it. Stomach samples from dead loons, the few cases of seeing food brought to the surface, and a few studies of captive loons form the basis for most of our knowledge in this area.

Loons are sight feeders. They lower their heads into the water as they swim and when they see

something they want to pursue, they dive. Looking into the water is called peering, and it is used not only when fishing, but also during social interactions. Loons regularly look into the water even when there doesn't appear to be any reason. I suppose if we lived in between the two mediums of water and air and needed to know what was going on in both, we would do the same.

Loons can pursue fish to great depths, but most of their feeding occurs in surprisingly shallow water. I found that adult loons fishing for themselves preferred parts of lakes with water depths of three to six feet. It shouldn't be all that surprising because the majority of fish in a lake are in the

littoral zone or the part of the lake where rooted plants can grow to the surface. The adults fed in other deeper parts of the lake as well, but used them infrequently. Interestingly, we often see loons feeding in the deeper parts of lakes with lots of lakeshore cottages and recreational use. I suspect they are pushed away from their favored feeding areas by all of the noise and traffic.

Being sight feeders, loons need adequate light to see. Thus, they do much of their feeding at times of day when sunlight penetrates the water most deeply. Feeding occurs throughout the day, but may be timed to correspond when fish move into shallow areas from the deeper parts of the lake.

Loons prefer fish, but live on lakes

with varying amounts and kinds of fish. Therefore, they have become opportunistic feeders, eating whatever is easiest to catch and most abundant. In many of the lakes they occupy across Canada and the northern United States, yellow perch seem to be the favored species. Yellow perch can be quite abundant, live mostly within ten to fifteen feet of the surface, are large enough to provide a good meal but small enough to eat whole, and have a zig-zag swimming pattern that loons find easy for pursuit. On lakes without yellow perch, loons will eat just about any other fish of the right size. What they prefer, however, are small, slow-moving fish without spines or hard bony plates and with small heads.

Fish are not the only food for loons. They regularly eat crayfish and a variety of aquatic invertebrates. We know they eat crabs on the wintering grounds, but we don't know how important they are as a food item.

How much loons eat has been a concern to fishermen. While we still don't know for sure, a 1973 study of captive loons by University of Guelph researcher Jack Barr suggests that a loon family of four may eat more than a ton of fish over the course of a summer. While that sounds like a lot of fish, it is a small proportion of the fish in a healthy lake of one hundred acres or more.

When a loon chases a fish underwater, its wings are held tightly to the

side and the head bobs back and forth with each stroke of the foot. As a fish turns, the loon turns by thrusting one foot to the side. Sometimes, the wings are spread slightly for stability or ruddering. The head is thrust forward at the last moment to catch the fish, which is held crosswise in the bill. Loons do not use their wings for propulsion underwater when they are feeding. However, I have seen them use their wings when they were frightened and trying to escape quickly.

The average length of a feeding dive is less than a minute although loons have the ability to stay underwater for perhaps as long as five minutes. Short dives of ten seconds or less are too short to produce a fish in most instances and are probably part of a social display.

Loons catch fish of various sizes. The optimal sized fish is probably six to eight inches long. Many folks have seen loons choke down much larger fish, and I once watched a loon swallow a fish that was at least fifteen inches long. It took that loon a good ten minutes to work the fish all the way down inch by inch, and the tail of the fish was still flapping just before it disappeared down the gullet.

Even the most basic routines of loons are interesting to avid loon watchers. Fortunately, loons have far more complicated and intriguing behaviors and communication techniques to keep us all entertained.

Loon Music

Loons use a combination of vocalizations and displays to send messages to other loons. On the northern breeding lakes, the messages often have to do with defense of a territory, mate, or chick. Scientists have studied the context of the calls and ritualistic behaviors and can assign certain generalized messages to them. Continued research in this area has resulted in further unraveling of the complex messages loons use.

Common loons give five basic calls. Loon chicks peep when they are begging for food. The peeps can be accompanied by pecks to the bill, neck, or head of the adult. Sometimes, loon chicks raise themselves nearly out of the water as they excitedly peck at a parent.

Adult loons give the hoot, wail, tremolo, and yodel and combinations of the tremolo and wail and of the tremolo and yodel. Each of the basic calls has distinct variations that allow for more specific messages within the general context of the basic message.

The hoot is the simplest loon call consisting of one short note. The pitch and the volume of the note vary and may alter the nature of the message. We know very little about the meaning of this call and presume that it is a contact call used when loons are in close proximity. Hoots are the most common call given when groups of loons are interacting peacefully.

The wail is a long, drawn-out call that sounds like the howl of a wolf. It is almost mournful in its quality and people have thought it to be a loon saddened by a lost mate. In reality it is used to bring two loons that are far apart closer together. A loon that is on its nest incubating eggs may wail to bring its mate closer so that a nest exchange can be made. Other times, adult loons wail to one another to maintain contact when they are too far apart to see. A member of a mated pair that has flown to a nearby lake to feed might be called back by its mate. A wail given by one adult to the other almost always results in a responding wail. Parent loons wail to their chicks to get them off the nest, when they are bringing food, and to get them to come out of the shoreline weeds when they have been hiding.

Wail calls can be of one, two, or three notes and the volume of the call can be varied. Loud, three note wails are thought to send the most urgent message and soft, one note calls the least. Adults wail softly to each other in a call that sounds like a mew during courtship.

I often saw bald eagles flying over the lakes on my study area in northern Maine. When loons noticed eagles, they would give a wail that sounded slightly different from other wails. After hearing this variation a number of times, I could predict the presence of an eagle just by the calls the loons gave. Loons did not respond to other large birds such as ospreys, gulls, ravens, and large hawks.

Tremolos and yodels tend to be used in association with body postures and motions. The tremolo is the staccato set of high and low notes that sounds like a maniacal laugh. Bill Barklow, then a researcher at Tufts University, was the first to study and describe the meanings of tremolo calls. He found that loons give three types of tremolos, which all gave the same message, but at different intensities. The calls were given when loons were disturbed at their nest or with their young or when a loon spotted a person nearby. The tremolo seemed to serve as an alarm. Typically, loons giving a tremolo move away from the source of the disturbance whether it is a person or another loon.

A tremolo is the most frequently given call in flight, and it is recognizable by its different pace. Sometimes, a mated pair will fly off a lake together and give the flight tremolo in an alternating duet. More often, the flight tremolo is given by a single loon flying over a lake occupied by other loons. We think it may be used as a query to the loons below. If no response is given, it may be that the loons on the water will not act aggressively. Flight tremolos probably aren't confined to

being questions to loons below because they are given in other contexts. I used to hear flight tremolos given by several loons at the same time just after dawn as the loons flew between Lake May and Leech Lake in Walker, Minnesota. From my bed, I wondered what they might mean when given over land.

Anyone who has watched loons on their nesting lakes knows that loons act differently when they are together than when they are apart. When a loon sees another loon approaching, it often stretches its neck higher in an alert posture. If the approaching loon is its mate, the neck is shortened and the two birds swim by each other, pointing their heads and bills slightly to the outside. The bill is a formidable weapon, and by watching what loons do with it when meeting another loon, one can start to determine the nature of the interaction.

If the approaching loon is an intruder to the territory, both loons may have their necks in the alert position and they may circle each other after the initial pass. Tremolos are often given at this time. Peering into the water may be followed by rapid dives loon biologists call "jerk dives" because of the jerky motion. More agitation may lead to "splash dives" in which one or both loons hurl their entire bodies into the water making big splashes. These behaviors are not limited to only two loons, but can occur in large and small groups as well.

Both the male and female get involved with territorial defense displays although the male seems to do so more frequently. Sometimes, intruders leave after just a brief interaction with the territory holders. Other times, displays that show a higher level of aggression ensue. One of these displays is a surface rush in which the aggressor holds its wings to the sides, points its bill forward, and rushes across the water at the intruder. The body can be held low to the water or the loon can appear to be running across the water with its body nearly erect. Occasionally, two loons will square off in the same posture.

I have often witnessed another display that may serve to let off some aggression without actual combat. It generally occurs after loons in a group have been feeding or interacting socially. The group seems to become more agitated as two or more of them swim in a small circle and take turns alternately diving and peering into the water in a routine known as a "circle dance." A dozen or more loons may engage in this display in which one loon makes a short dive of ten to fifteen seconds while the others peer underwater to watch. Other loons may dive while the first is still below the surface.

The agitation level grows as the dives become more frequent and rapid.

Eventually two of the loons break off from the group and begin rowing with their wings across the water. One seems to be chasing the other, following ten feet or so behind, but never catching up to the loon in the lead. The lead loon rows in a zig-zag pattern and the chaser follows. I have watched these chases go on for more than five minutes until the aggression wanes or the birds tire out or both. During the chase, both birds give the tremolo call over and over again at a rapid pace.

Yodels are associated with the highest level of aggression. They are the call that sounds like a series of high and low notes given in a series of repeated phrases. Only male loons yodel, and each male loon has his own individual, identifiable yodel, which he keeps apparently unchanged his entire adult life.

Yodels are given during territorial encounters. The longer the call and the more series of repeated phrases given, the more aggressive and intense the encounter. I have heard a male loon give thirteen of the repeated phrases in one call. He did it twice on a large lake in Ontario just a week after the ice went out and was calling at another loon close by, which I presumed to be an intruding male. Ed Miller, then researcher at Ohio State University, has seen male loons give the yodel while flying between lakes. Perhaps these are males defending multiple lake territories.

The highest level of aggression short of actual fighting is usually between two male loons disputing a territory ownership or boundary. Males square off in either a flattened posture on the water surface or with their bodies elevated and their wings held out to the side. One or both give the yodel call until one quits and goes away or the encounter escalates and a fight starts. In a fight, loons use their bills and stab at each other. Serious injuries and even death have been witnessed by scientists and casual observers alike, though fights are far less common than the displays.

Lauren Wentz studied the calls loons give at night in an attempt to understand the significance of the beautiful nocturnal choruses heard throughout the summer. Her study took place primarily in the Sylvania Wilderness Area in Michigan's Upper Peninsula. I accompanied her a few nights when she set up fancy recording equipment on shore and recorded the loon calls throughout the night.

Lauren found that most night choruses start with a wail from one loon. Wails, tremolos, and yodels are given throughout the night, but tremolo duets are the most common call. Her interpretation was that the pair calls to advertise their presence on their territory and the fact that they are together. This may serve to strengthen the pair bond and to keep intruders away.

King of the Hill

When a pair of loons stakes out their territorial claim to a lake or part of it, they pronounce themselves lord and master of all they can see. Not only do they fend off the advances of rival loons who would have the place for their own, but they often make life miserable for other animals living there.

Because they are large, usually the largest swimming creature on the lake, they assert their dominance by bold intimidation. The sight of a loon swimming nearby can cause a family of ducks to move hurriedly along the shoreline to another cove or even up onto land. Muskrats plow a furious "vee" of water and head back to the safety of their grass houses when confronted by loons. Although they clearly intimidate some other animals, loons don't always use their power. Life on a lake can actually appear rather peaceful much of the time. However, this is a fragile harmony that can be disrupted at any moment.

Not all of the aquatic denizens are easily daunted. Beavers, one of the only animals that can match the loon's size, do not shy away from confrontations with loons. Many people have witnessed face-to-face sparring matches between the two. One wonderful sequence was captured on film by Peter Roberts, a nature photographer and film maker, from Washington. While filming loons in north-central Minnesota near Walker, Peter observed

a loon and beaver establishing aquatic turf. The two circled each other and took turns being the aggressor. The beaver lunged and slapped its fleshy tail while the loon postured with spread wings and dove. No clear victor emerged and neither seemed the worse for the wear. Later, however, the loon was noted to have broken off the tip of its lower mandible, perhaps in the action.

Boldness is not the loon's only *modus operandi*. Stealth is used very effectively to both scare and kill. Mother ducks with a line of ducklings in tow have much to fear. Numerous accounts of loons submerging at a distance and swimming to a brood of ducklings have been reported in the scientific and popular literature. Typically, the ducklings disappear as they are pulled below the surface and

are killed, but are not eaten. Larger ducklings and adults are killed by a powerful thrust of the loon's sharp bill into the abdomen.

Two outstanding photographs of a common loon killing a duckling were published along with a short story about the attack in *Alaska* magazine in 1980. Gary Musgrave was photographing a brood of mergansers with their mother in Alaska when a nearby loon suddenly

surfaced next to the brood and snatched a duckling, crushing it in its bill.

Many such reports come from western Minnesota where the range of the common goldeneye overlaps with areas of loon abundance. In the area around Bemidji, Minnesota Department of Natural Resources waterfowl biologists report many cases in which loons have killed off entire broods of goldeneyes. Other kinds of ducks killed by loons in various parts of the world include mallards, ring-necked ducks, common eiders, red-breasted mergansers, and oldsquaws.

Even Canada geese, which are large and aggressive birds, are vulnerable to attacks from loons. In the early 1970s, Wisconsin DNR waterfowl researcher Mike Zicus reported one such incident

in northwestern Wisconsin at Crex Meadows Wildlife Management Area. There, a pair of loons harassed a family of two adult geese and their three young goslings and eventually killed one of the goslings despite the best protective efforts of the parent geese.

While the duck-killing behavior of loons is not common and widespread, it happens often enough to make scientists wonder what purpose it plays in the life of loons. So far, no good explanation has come forth. Even if we do not understand why it occurs, it serves to demonstrate the aggressive side of the loon's personality.

During my studies of loons in northern Maine, several times I witnessed a loon submerge far out in the lake and resurface in the shallows right next to a great blue heron fishing there. The explosion of water just behind the heron caused it to squawk hoarsely and to get its gangly body airborne.

Aquatic animals are not the only ones harassed by loons. One of my field technicians watched a pair of loons on Snowshoe Lake swim quickly across the lake to follow and bother a black bear that had decided to swim across the lake rather than circumnavigate it.

Unbeknownst to me at the time, Bill Barklow (then at Framingham State University), who pioneered much of the research on loon calls, and June Chamberlain from Tufts University had watched a curious interaction on the same lake between a group of loons and a coyote.

Published in the scientific journal *Journal of Field Ornithology*, their account reported a group of ten loons interacting socially on the lake. A coyote appeared on shore and began to swim across the lake. When it was about a football field away from the group, one of the loons gave the tremolo call, and the coyote veered toward the group. The coyote tried to catch the loons as they called, swam, and dove around it. After a few minutes, the coyote moved away from the loon group, but some of them continued to harass it. Before it could reach shore, it became fatigued and drowned.

I am not the only person to have swum with loons close by, but I had one up close and personal experience that convinced me of the loon's superior attitude toward other creatures in or on the water. After one particularly long, buggy, and hot day doing field research on Millinocket Lake in northern Maine, I decided to take a swim before retiring for the night. Between me and the orange blaze of the setting sun, about 500 feet out in the lake, was a group of a dozen or so loons swimming and diving peacefully. I skinny dipped that night knowing no one else was around and swam a short distance out into the lake.

I could hear the loons hooting to each other, but being nearsighted and without my glasses, I couldn't see just where they were. Suddenly, I realized that the group was moving toward me, and they weren't all that far away. I tread water for several minutes as the loons came closer and closer. Soon they were all around me and the closest ones were no more than ten feet away. Eye-to-eye they looked a lot bigger than when I was in a boat at a distance. They dove around underwater, and all I could think of was that I didn't have on a bathing suit. As they dove and resurfaced, I thought they might be looking to see how much of the strange creature was underwater. After a few minutes, the loon group swam away to check out things far more interesting than a naked man in the water. To this day, some ten years later, I recall the feeling that remained as I climbed out of the lake. In the lake, the loons' element, I was a far inferior creature and they treated me as royalty might treat peasantry, with mild curiosity, but mostly indifference.

Loons walk the fine line of many territorial creatures. They must stake a claim to an area to protect adequate food supply, nest sites, and other needs. At the same time, maintaining these areas takes its toll in the form of energy they must expend. And the aggressive motives create a more dangerous lifestyle. Injuries and even death are possible outcomes.

Loons are enigmatic in this sense—they appear stately and serene. Their aggressive nature seems almost out of place. But this is the nature of the beast. Millennia of evolutionary change have wrought this bird from its more primitive ancestors. The trade-offs of this lifestyle have served it well. Like so many other traits, we must come to know, understand, and accept it for how it serves the loon.

Neighborhoods

Our early notions of loon society led us to think that loons were solitary birds on their breeding grounds and that they defended discrete territories. We essentially thought loons were loners. As more and more research has been conducted, however, we find that loon society is as complicated as a soap opera.

Loon biologists now feel certain that loon society is somewhat akin to human neighborhoods. Loons on their territories react more aggressively to tape recordings of the yodels of male loons from far away than they do to those of nearby loons. They seem to recognize the voices of their neighbors as less threatening.

Life in the "hood" is not orderly. Results of banding studies in which individual loons can be identified have shown that territory owners can change both within a year as well as between years. So far, it is usually the female who switches partners. Apparently, there are always loons testing the strength of the pair bond between territorial breeding pairs and testing the ability of a male loon to defend his watery homestead.

Researchers have not yet figured out the circumstances under which territories have changes in ownership. The most common factor so far seems to be a nest failure, but I suspect that other forces may come into play, such as the age of the birds, their physical fitness, and their experience.

When I began my studies of loons in 1982, I was not prepared for the far from simple patterns of loon society. I went to several large lakes in northern Maine, each with six or more nesting pairs of loons, expecting to be able to map the territory boundaries based on the movements of loons within their

territories and aggressive confrontations near the boundaries. What I found instead was far beyond my understanding.

Although there were nesting pairs, the territories seemed not to exist, at least not in the way I expected. Trespass was rampant. The locations of territorial boundary disputes varied. And there were many more loons on the lake than just the territorial pairs.

Over the course of three summers of recording the daily activities of loons on three lakes, I learned that loons on large lakes lived a far different lifestyle than those on small lakes with room for just one pair. While the pairs on small lakes had their homes to themselves most of the summer, those on the large lakes were involved with nonaggressive social interactions with other loons an average of 17 percent of the time. To my surprise, my technicians and I saw the 16 pairs of loons on the large lakes engage in aggressive territorial displays only 97 times in three years.

Many large lakes, particularly in areas with high loon populations, have small or large groups of adult loons that are not members of a breeding pair. They move around to nearby lakes throughout the summer, and on any one day, several or all of them may be in an identifiable group. Loon biologists refer to members of these groups as "floaters."

Floaters are adult loons who do

74

not have territories or mates. They are capable of breeding and sometimes take over a territory during the summer or in a future year. Floaters arrive soon after the territorial pairs in the spring and stay on the lakes until fall migration. Not all members of a floater group are nonbreeders. Occasionally, a member of a breeding pair from a small nearby lake flies to a large lake to feed and joins the group for a time.

Peter Croskery, a biologist from Ontario, studied summer loon flocks on several large lakes northeast of Lake Superior. On one lake, the flock numbered 60 floaters! As on my study lakes, the birds stayed primarily in the main open-water basin of the lakes. They frequently broke down into smaller groups. At times, individuals or small groups flew off to nearby lakes to feed.

Floater groups trespass into the territories of nesting pairs frequently. During the incubation period, the loon not on the nest typically joins the group and interacts nonaggressively with them. The group swims together, and it appears that the territorial loon tries to lead them out of the area. At times, the peaceful nature of the group becomes agitated and aggressive displays occur. Occasionally, both members of a territorial pair will join the group, particularly in late summer.

After the chicks have hatched, the floater groups pose a threat to the territorial pairs. When they approach a territory boundary or a nursery area, the pair moves out to intercept them and escort them away. The chicks are often sent into the weeds along the shoreline where they wait until they are retrieved by the adults.

Floater loons sometimes kill young loon chicks. In New Hampshire, where volunteer and summer intern loon watchers keep close track of most of the loons in the state, so called "rogue loons" sneak into the territories of nesting pairs and kill the chicks when they are left unattended. The purpose of these attacks is related to natural selection and is a common occurrence in the animal world. For example, male lions that take over a pride immediately kill the cubs who were sired by the ousted male.

Loons occupy a wide variety of nesting lakes. Some are small and can support just one pair of loons. On these, summer is quiet with few intruders. Some lakes are too small to meet all of the requirements, but when small lakes are clustered on the landscape as they are in many parts of Maine, Minnesota, northeastern Wisconsin, and parts of Canada, loon pairs will claim two or three small lakes as their summer home. Loons in this situation face a much more difficult time in keeping other loons out of their territories and adopt a different patrolling routine. Loons on large lakes with large open-water basins in the middle have to share the lake with other territorial pairs and floater groups. They have many more social interactions and are less aggressive.

It is probably advantageous for loons to be territorial and to try to exclude other loons from preferred nesting, chick rearing, and feeding areas. However, the size and shape of the lake and the proximity to other lakes may determine their approach.

On small lakes occupied by just one pair, aggressive territoriality may pay off because of the low visitation rates from other loons. On large lakes with several pairs and floaters, extreme territoriality may not be advantageous. Territory perimeters may be mostly open water and difficult to defend. Reacting to visitation from other individuals and groups might occupy most of the owners' time. Instead, nesting pairs on large lakes may maintain nonaggressive social relations with their neighbors and visitors. This may pay off in reducing social strife and in having access to good feeding areas outside of the cores of their territories.

Loon society is more complex than we ever believed and is determined in part by local conditions. Loons have shown remarkable flexibility in adapting to the varied habitats they occupy.

CHAPTER 4

The Endless Cycle

The story of a loon's life can only be told in the context of natural cycles. Time passes, seasons wax and wane, years come and go. The cycle seems endless. The life of an individual loon is a thread that enters the cycle when the loon is born and exits when the loon dies. The threads that are all loons are woven into a tapestry with a recognizable pattern that repeats itself year after year.

North to Open Water

We enter the cycle in March. Loons that have been wintering along the Atlantic, Pacific, and Gulf coasts of North America have just grown new wing feathers to carry them to their breeding grounds to the north. Drab winter plumage is being replaced by breeding colors and patterns. Not all loons are acquiring spring finery, however. Loons less than four years old replace their winter colors with less than spectacularly colored feathers. Only when they reach adulthood at four years will they wear the familiar black and white pattern we see on northern lakes.

Increasing day length makes the loons restless, and they make short flights up and down the coasts. This migratory restlessness seen in many creatures is called *zugenruhe*, a term coined by German scientists studying animal behavior. Eventually, the loons move northward along the coasts joining other loons in large, loose flocks as they gather or "stage" for a great migration across land.

No one knows for certain what paths loons take from their wintering areas to northern lakes. Their ability to fly very fast and to go great distances in a day probably limits the number of stops they need to make. Some loons have to fly only short distances, for example, those loons breeding on lakes in New England and the Canadian Maritimes. Mid-continental breeding populations, however, must journey overland hundreds if not thousands of miles.

Casual observations of spring migration combined with intensive observations in certain areas give us a rough idea of how things go. In the Upper Midwest, loons start showing up on lakes, reservoirs, and large rivers in late March and early April. They appear singly or in large or small groups. As the ice disappears from lakes south of their breeding area, they push forward. Finally, when the ice clears from a breeding lake, territorial loons arrive and stake their claims. People report seeing loons flying over still frozen lakes once or several times a day just days before the ice goes out. If a small, open lead of water appears, they may set down and wait for the rest of the ice to go. It appears that in some areas loons follow the line of open lakes, scouting the lakes to the north as they open.

This is not the only migratory pattern used by loons. Scientists observing the spring migration of birds in the Great Lakes region have found that there are days when thousands of loons fly across these inland seas. The Whitefish Point Bird Observatory on the southeastern shore of Lake Superior has kept detailed records of spring bird migration for many years. Trained observers huddle in parkas and sleeping bags and lean back in lawn chairs to count ducks, hawks, loons, and other birds as they pass by overhead. Every year, usually around the end of April and the beginning of May,

the phenomenon begins and lasts for about two weeks.

The identity of these Great Lakes migrants is unknown, but they are probably loons nesting in the interior of Canada. By late April, when this pulse of migrants appears, loons nesting in Minnesota, Wisconsin, and Michigan, have been on their breeding lakes for one to three weeks. However, ice-out on lakes in northern Ontario, Manitoba, and Quebec has not happened yet. It seems certain that the loons still passing through are heading to those areas.

The urge to return north is strong and the loons hurry along. Because each lake or part of it is claimed for a territory, arriving first is advantageous. There could be a mad scramble for every lake, but loons seem to sort things out by returning to the same lakes each year. This was widely assumed for many years, but it was only with the ability to identify individual loons that it has been confirmed as a widespread phenomenon.

Judith McIntyre, one of the pioneers of loon research and a leading authority on loons world-wide, was the first to demonstrate loons returning to the same lake in consecutive years. In 1972, near Roseau in northwestern Minnesota, Judy captured and attached wing and leg markers to an adult common loon. The next year, the loon returned to the same lake with the tags still intact. Some loons captured incidentally during waterfowl banding operations near Bemidji, Minnesota, and banded have been seen on the same lakes in subsequent years.

These few instances of banded loons returning to the same lakes guided our thinking for over a decade. It wasn't until the late 1980s and early 1990s that we gathered a large enough body of evidence to confirm that most loons return to the same lake year after year. This was a major breakthrough in our understanding of loons.

The reason it took so long to get this kind of information is that loons are difficult to catch on the water, and although they would have been relatively easy to catch at the nest site, we never wanted to disturb them. Judy McIntyre and the waterfowl banders in Minnesota caught loons by shining a spotlight at them from a boat at night and approaching close enough to net them with a long-handled fishing net. This seemed to work well only on shallow lakes on which the loons could be seen as they dove underwater to avoid the nets. It never worked well enough for anyone to invest the time to try to catch large numbers of loons.

In the late 1980s, on the Turtle-Flambeau Flowage in northeastern Wisconsin, Jerry Belant (University of Wisconsin—Stevens Point researcher) captured several loons using this method. He marked the loons with standard aluminum U.S. Fish and Wildlife leg bands and wing tags similar to the ones used by Judy. He also attached colored plastic leg bands that I created in 1982. These could be seen when loons took off in flight and when they did the foot waggle movement. Jerry's loons did not always return to the same territory they occupied the previous year. This information was the first hint that not all loons conform to the same behavior.

During the 1990s, Dave Evers perfected the technique of capturing loons using the nightlighting method. Working primarily on the Seney National Wildlife Refuge in the eastern part of Michigan's Upper Peninsula, Dave found that there is a short period of time when adult loons can be caught fairly easily. During the time the chicks are around four weeks old, Dave captured chicks and found that the adults would stay close to the capture boat while the chicks were being measured and weighed. Over the past few years, Dave and his capture crews have exploited the adult loons' vulnerability to capture at this time and have captured and marked hundreds of adult loons in the United States and Canada. His sample of marked loons is by far the largest ever assembled.

Dave and his crews have banded approximately 700 common loons since 1988, around 400 adults and 300 chicks. He has found that about 80 percent of the banded adults return to the same territory they occupied the year before, but they don't every year and they don't always have the same mate. Sometimes, a territory holder doesn't return one year, but does the next.

Much more mate switching occurs than we thought. Apparently, nest failure often leads to a weakening of the pair bond and sometimes abandonment of the territory by one or both adults. New mates are found and the second nesting attempt for a loon pair in a territory may well be with one of the old pair and a new bird.

Another less intrusive method for identifying individual loons was being developed in the 1980s by Ed Miller from Governor's State University near Chicago. For many years, researchers had noted that male loons sometimes could be told apart by the pattern of the notes in their yodel call. Ed looked into this more deeply and found that tape recordings of the yodels of male loons could be displayed on paper and that clear, distinct patterns could be seen. He was so sure of what he was seeing that he took a sample of the paper "sound spectrographs" to a local school and asked young schoolchildren to go through them and separate them into piles of similar yodels based on the patterns they could see. He did not tell them how many piles there should be or how many should go in each pile.

Yet, the children were able to separate them into groups with 100 percent accuracy!

Ed perfected the technique of getting male loons to give their yodel call so he could record them on tape. When he had become very proficient at it, he asked me to accompany him on a recording mission. As we launched our small boat into a northern Michigan lake, Ed explained the technique. I listened with great interest, but resigned myself to slight skepticism in case it didn't work. Not only did it work, but the loons behaved just as Ed said they would. It seemed as if a script had been played out with the actors reciting their lines perfectly. I left, a firm

believer in Ed's ability to get the loons to talk to him.

In his study area in and around the Sylvania Wilderness Area in the western Upper Peninsula of Michigan, Ed expanded his sample of loons so that he could look at rates of territory reoccupancy on a much larger scale. He found that after several years, average reoccupancy rates were about 95 percent. So, most male loons did return to the same lakes each year. What Ed, Dave Evers, and others are learning, however, is that loon society is different than we thought. While this has shattered our concept of perfect fidelity to mates and lakes, it has helped us understand the complexity of the loon's world.

Setting Up Shop

The reason loons come to north-ern lakes is to find a place to nest and raise young. Their requirements are fairly simple: the lake must be large enough for take-offs and landings; it must have fish or aquatic insects for food; the water must be clear enough for the loons to see their prey; there must be an accessible place on the shoreline or on an island for the nest; and the water level must be relatively stable during the nesting period.

A large proportion of the research on loons has been on the characteristics of lakes they occupy. We have been obsessed with trying to understand why loons choose the lakes they do. Yet, after twenty years, it is still somewhat of a mystery. We can describe loon habitat in general terms, but there always seem to be many exceptions when we try to get too specific. After nearly thirteen years of studying loons, reading research reports, and talking to the amateur and professional loon observers, I have come to look at loon habitat differently than most people.

What I see is this. Loons have general needs for nesting, feeding, and access to lakes. The waters of northern North America, Europe, and Asia present loons with a wide variety of choices for meeting these criteria. Some are better for one factor than others. In a general way, some lakes are better for all factors than others. Regardless of the lake a loon pair chooses, there are pros

and cons. A lake with abundant prey may also have more abundant predators that would threaten loon chicks. A large lake with many potential breeding territories may have ample food and nesting areas, but the social strife may be high. A small, isolated lake may be peaceful, but its food resources may be limited once in a while. Small lakes may also be difficult for loons to take off from. This perspective keeps me from trying to characterize ideal loon habitat. Like most things in Nature, choosing a nesting lake for loons is selecting among trade-offs.

Loons tend to return to their nesting lakes singly. Typically, the male arrives first and defends the lake from other males who are looking to set up new territories. The female arrives seven

What happens when one of the loon pair dies between one nesting season and the next? There are a few documented cases of marked loons in which one of the sexes did not return. Typically, new mates are found quickly.

Competition for the breeding territories is keen, particularly in parts of the loon's range where the population is high. In Ontario, where there are tens of thousands of loons, a small experiment was done to determine whether territories would be reoccupied if the territorial pair was removed. In each case, the vacant territory was quickly occupied by a new pair. We suspect that loons filling in vacant territories are part of a pool of unpaired and non-territorial adults that move around in large or small loose groups during the summer.

By mid-May in the United States, most loon pairs have re-established their claim to a lake and are in the process of courtship and initiation of nesting. Courtship is a rather subtle set of synchronized swimming, diving, and calling behaviors. Some people confuse the excited loud calling and splashing of aggression with courtship. The innocuous courtship displays can be missed by all but the most observant loon-watcher.

Courtship culminates in breeding and the subsequent selection of a nest site. When the female is receptive to breeding, the male swims near the shoreline giving a gentle mew call and turning his head to the side. This is an

to ten days after the male. In northern Canada and in years when ice-out is delayed, males and females may arrive at the same time, but there is no evidence of loons flying to lakes in pairs. Thus, we suspect that loons show greater fidelity to the lakes than they do to their mates. Having the same mate for many years is a by-product of both sexes returning to the same lakes independently.

invitation to mate. The female typically ignores the male several times before climbing onto the shore. The male follows and stands on the female's back while they make cloacal contact. Copulation lasts anywhere from two to fifteen minutes, but averages three to ten. After they have mated, the male returns to the water and preens his feathers while the female stays on land for a few minutes. She may choose the mating site as a place to nest. If that is the case, she picks at the dead grasses, leaves, and twigs nearby and starts making the nest. In many cases, however, the nest site is in a different location.

Our fancy for trying to understand why loons nest where they do has been as great as that for how they choose nesting lakes. Numerous studies have looked at the size, structure, placement, and orientation of nests. From these, no clear picture emerges, but as with their selection of lakes, there seem to be a few generalities that apply in most cases.

Loons always choose a nest site close to the water's edge to reduce the distance they have to travel. Rarely will a nest be more than a foot or two from the water when it is first constructed. Sometimes, water levels in the lakes recede leaving a nest tens of feet from the water, and a loon may have to shuffle slowly over rocks and mud to reach its nest. Nest sites near deep water are generally considered superior to those adjacent to shallow water. Apparently, the risk of predation of the eggs is lessened when loons can slip away from their nests quietly underwater.

Loons seem to prefer small islands as nest sites. Study after study has shown a clear preference for islands. We believe that small islands afford a lesser chance of predators finding the nest site. Mainland nests are often predated by skunks and raccoons, particularly on lakes where people are present and these small predators enjoy increased population levels. Yet, not all sites are on islands, even when islands are present. Clearly, it is not always one way and there may very well be other factors more important than predation.

On my study area in northern Maine, I found that loons living on large lakes with six or more territorial pairs per lake liked to locate their nests in narrow, slow-moving inlet or outlet streams called "deadwaters." Their success in hatching eggs in these locations was actually higher than on islands. I speculated that the deadwaters gave loons a place where the incubating adult would not be disturbed by the many groups of non-territorial loons that were always cruising around the lake.

Regardless of where the nests are located, they tend to be used year after year. I looked at nest locations for loons on a variety of lakes in Maine

and New Hampshire and discovered a strong affinity for using either the same nest or the area within close proximity of the nest nearly every year. This traditional use of nest sites is not surprising for a bird that occupies a relatively stable environment, returns to the same lake most years, and may live to be twenty or thirty years old in the wild.

Loons construct their nests out of a variety of materials using whatever is present at the nest site. Typically, the nest is comprised of dead vegetation and a little bit of mud. However, all of us who have studied loons on their nesting lakes have good stories of really unusual sites. I have seen nests made in depressions in sandy beaches and eggs laid directly on rocks as well as in more "normal" places. The one that takes the cake for me was on a small island on Millimigasset Lake in northern Maine. This rocky islet had almost no vegetation on it and a pair of herring gulls had laid their three eggs in a nest made out of freshwater mussel shells. The loons waited until the gulls had moved their young into the water before they took over the nest site and used it to successfully hatch two young. The mussel shells were on the rocks because otters living in the lake used the island as a feeding site and left the remains of many a meal there.

Once the nest is made, the female lays one, two, or very rarely, three eggs. Two is the normal clutch size for loons in their first nesting attempt of the year. The eggs are laid one at a time over the course of two or three days. The female begins incubating them as soon as the first one is laid so that one egg is always a day or so ahead of the other in development.

Periodically, the eggs are turned to prevent the embryo from sticking to the shell.

Loons use a strategy of sitting on the eggs almost all of the time to maximize the probability that they will hatch. Unlike many other birds, loons do not build nests that are well concealed. In fact, most loon nests I have seen stand out like a sore thumb on the shoreline. However, a loon sitting on its eggs is too large a bird for gulls, crows, or ravens to harass. Occasionally, eggs will be left uncovered for several minutes to an hour or more while the adults relax or feed in the water nearby, but most loons are on the nest throughout the incubation period.

A variety of predators keep their eyes open for a meal of loon eggs. Besides large birds like ravens and gulls, mink, skunks, and raccoons are known loon nest predators. Rarely is an adult loon killed at the nest despite its vulnerability. Surprisingly, mink, which are much smaller than loons, have been known to kill adult loons while they incubated.

Many of the first nest attempts fail. On some lakes with several pairs of loons, some years produce no chicks at all. Loons have adapted to predation in part by the ability to produce a second set of eggs, and in rare instances, a third. Renest attempts typically are not in the same nest as the first. Instead, loons choose an alternate nest site somewhere else in their nesting territory. On my study area, I knew of a second and sometimes a third nest site in most of the territories. Researchers have also noted that an alternate nest site may be used in the year after one in which the nest attempt failed.

When an initial nest fails, a renest attempt will occur about half of the

time. Second nests have only one egg in them more often than initial nests, perhaps because of the high energy investment of producing such large eggs. Renests only occur when a nest is destroyed, not after chicks hatch and subsequently die. After hatching, some sort of behavioral switch seems to be thrown and there is no going back to try nesting again.

Both adults share incubation duties. Because the sexes are nearly

and was returning to the portage trail when I heard a male loon give the yodel call.

I swung the canoe around and looked for the male who should have been in the classic "crouch and yodel" posture. Instead, all I saw was one loon sitting rather quietly on the water. As I watched, the male yodeled again and try as I might, I could not spot him on the water. I dug out my binoculars and scanned the far shoreline thinking I might have missed seeing him in the shaded area, but he wasn't there. On the third yodel, I spotted him. He was sitting on the nest and was yodeling loudly with his head held down close to the water.

He eventually left the nest and I paddled over to it to look at the eggs. One was hatching as I watched and I could hear a faint peeping from the other. This was the first, and to my knowledge, the only case of a male loon yodeling from the nest and the only evidence that a male loon might be the one on the nest as the chicks hatch.

After twenty-eight or so days of incubation, the first loon chick pecks its way out of the shell. It has already begun to make soft peeping calls while still in the egg. Its sibling emerges a day or two later. The chicks are not kept at the nest for long. As soon as their soot-colored downy plumage is dry, they are taken from the nest into the water where they will spend most of the rest of their life.

impossible to tell apart, we aren't sure if one parent incubates more than the other. A chance observation I made one day clarified that the male does sit on the nest during critical periods. I had been canoeing in Millimigasset Lake

Raising a Family

Hatching of the chicks is an important benchmark in the loon's breeding season. All attention is shifted away from the nest and the loon family focuses on getting the chicks to a stage where they can care for and feed themselves. Occasionally, one adult and the chicks will sit on the nest for a few hours during one of the first days after hatching, but for most loons, once off the nest it is forgotten until the next year.

Early researchers of loons knew that the young were taken away from the nest site to another part of the lake,

but it wasn't until Judy McIntyre's studies in Manitoba and mine in Maine that we gained an understanding of the importance of the areas used by loon families during the first few weeks of the chicks' lives.

Soon after the eggs hatch adult loons move away from the nest with the chicks in tow. The youngsters are very buoyant and are strong swimmers for their size. The twenty-eight days of incubation produces a well developed chick that can function in the water within hours of hatching. The loon chicks are taken to a part of the lake with special characteristics. We call these "nursery areas" because they

play an important role in the first two or three weeks of the chicks' development. Typically, a nursery area is in a sheltered bay or cove and has an abundance of small fish and aquatic insects that the adults can readily catch to feed the chicks. I found that adult loons did not use these same areas for feeding themselves, perhaps to avoid depleting the food resource upon which the chicks would depend. I also carefully mapped the locations of the nursery areas and found that loon pairs tended to use the same nurseries year after year. On small lakes, nurseries may not be distinguishable from other parts of the lake, but on large lakes like the ones in Maine on which I worked and the ones in Manitoba where Judy McIntyre studied nurseries, they are distinctly different and discrete areas.

Until recently, we knew very little about the first few days of a loon's life because researchers tended to keep their distance and tried to avoid disturbing the family group. Although various researchers had reported some aggression between loon chicks, we assumed that all was peaceful and that the adults spent their time feeding and caring for the young. It wasn't until 1988 that we learned something new. Gary Dulin, then a master's degree student at Central Michigan University, studied the early chick-rearing period of loons on Beaver Island in northern Lake Michigan. He observed loon families intensively and found that loon chicks engage in pecking battles the first few days after hatching and that the older and usually larger chick, the one that hatches first, wins all of the pecking battles. This allows the dominant chick to be fed first and to accept or refuse food items brought by the adults.

Back in 1907, William Beebe (a zoologist at Kansas State University) documented intense fighting between two captive loon chicks, but it wasn't until Gary Dulin's work that we understood the significance of the rivalry between siblings. Gary found that both chicks of a two-chick brood received approximately the same amounts of food during the first two weeks after hatching. Competition for food seemed to be lacking during that period. However, starting at two to three weeks after hatching, the dominant chick received most of the food, not because the adults selectively fed it, but because the dominant chick intimidated the

subordinate chick and swam first to the adult approaching with food. From that time on, the subordinate chick received a smaller and smaller proportion of the food brought by the adults and often, the subordinate chick died during the fifth or sixth week.

Dulin provided a logical explanation for the evolution and significance of this behavior. It appears that common loons are not always able to provide enough food to raise both chicks to fledging. The pecking battles establish a dominance hierarchy between the chicks so that in years in which enough food is not available, one chick will have an opportunity to survive instead of both chicks being equally fed and perishing. The competition for food gets keen at two to three weeks because chicks undergo increased energy demands caused by spending more time in the water, swimming greater distances, and starting a feather molt. The fifth or sixth week is a critical period because the juvenal contour feathers are rapidly replacing the down. Loon chicks may be growing

at their most rapid rate during these weeks, as well.

Sibling rivalry in loons occasionally produces unusually aggressive behavior. In 1986, on Virgin Lake in northern Wisconsin, Lorraine Hunsicker, a dedicated LoonWatch volunteer, watched a dominant loon chick so thoroughly beat up its younger sibling that the smaller chick was visibly injured and was continuously driven away from the family. It eventually disappeared and died. During all of the sibling battles, the adults watch calmly and do not interfere. Wildlife photographer Peter Roberts captured the intensity of these aggressive encounters and the apparent indifference of the adults on video tape. Despite my years of studying loons, I had never witnessed these battles and was shocked to see just how violent they were.

Adult loons do not seem to recognize the difference between the dominant and subordinate chicks and, similarly, they apparently do not recognize

their own chicks. In 1980, Ron Eckstein, a wildlife biologist with the Wisconsin Department of Natural Resources, took an orphaned loon chick to a lake with a loon family that had only one chick. The chick was accepted and grew to fledging. One of my field technicians, Rick Souza, saw a brood of three loon chicks on one of our study lakes that could only have been the result of natural brood mixing. While this is probably very uncommon, it pointed out that the adults tending the

large brood couldn't differentiate between their chicks and one from another pair and demonstrated additionally that loons can't count.

Young loons are vulnerable to predators, storms, and the chilling effects of cold northern lakes. Parents are able to minimize chick loss during the first few weeks after hatching by allowing chicks to ride on one or both of the adult's backs. This behavior reduces energy loss from chilling and protects the chicks from predators. Chicks are allowed to ride until they are seventeen to twenty-one days old. They may back-ride more than half of the day during the first eight days. After that, the percentage of the day spent back-riding decreases sharply until the adults no longer let the chicks climb aboard.

Loon chicks are tended almost constantly when they are very young, but the adults spend more and more time away from them as they get older. Usually, only one of the parents is gone at one time, but sometimes, circumstances arise that leave chicks on their own. These are typically the presence of people or of other loons in the loon territory. At these times, the chicks are often sent to shore to hide in beds of bulrushes or other emergent aquatic plants. There they stay crouched down on the water and silent until their parents come back for them.

I had the opportunity to watch just such an event one summer in northern

Maine. I was conducting a regular observation period on a pair of loons on Snowshoe Lake. There was a second territorial pair on the north end of the lake and a small flock of nonbreeding adults that usually hung out in the middle of the lake when they weren't flying to and from nearby Grand Lake Seboeis. The pair was feeding their two-week-old chicks in the nursery area when suddenly both adults gave warning calls and dove. The chicks moved quickly to shore and hid in the emergent vegetation. I could barely see them and they didn't move at all after getting there. Meanwhile, the adults swam to the edge of their territory where several other adults were swimming. They interacted with the intruders and swam across the lake over the course of the next half hour. I almost didn't notice, but one of the loons slipped away from the group and headed back toward the nursery, taking long underwater dives to get there. When the adult arrived, it swam slowly up and down the shoreline near where the chicks had gone and gave soft wail calls. I could still see the chicks, but they didn't move even when the adult passed right in front of them only twenty or thirty feet away. Finally, the chicks responded and rejoined their parent who had by that time been joined by the other adult.

Adult loons bring loon chicks all of their food for the first few weeks. Minnows, crayfish, and aquatic insects comprise most of the diet although occasionally small amounts of aquatic vegetation are consumed. The adults hold food items crosswise in their bills and the chicks take the food directly from them. The adults start to hold the food items underwater or drop them in the water after a few weeks and sometimes the fish that are brought are not killed, but stunned and the chicks must pick up food that moves. This gradual progression probably aids in the development of food capture skills. Loon chicks catch their first food on their own when they are around two or three weeks old, but they rely on their parents for almost all of their food until the end of the summer. The adults slowly wean the chicks and I suspect the chicks can feed themselves by the time they are eight to ten weeks old, but they stay with the adults hoping for continued free meals.

The sooty down the chicks have at hatching is replaced by a chocolate brown down after a couple of weeks. The first contour feathers like those worn by the adults start to emerge around three weeks. At five to six weeks of age, the chicks look ridiculously uncomfortable as the last of the down feathers are being molted.

The chicks grow quickly and noticeable changes in overall body size and bill length occur by three weeks. Chicks are nearly the size of the adults by eight weeks although they continue

to put on weight and their bill lengthens some after this time.

The maiden flights of loon chicks happen when they are ten to twelve weeks old. Their flight feathers are fully grown then and they strengthen their flight muscles by flapping their wings vigorously and by rowing across the surface of the lake. Young loons may fly to nearby large lakes where they congregate in the fall after the adult loons have left.

The loon family is together only three to four months. Over the course of the short northern summer, the adults must nest and raise chicks to the flight stage. They may have had late season snows on their backs in the spring as they established their nests and early fall frosts are turning the leaves crimson and gold just as their young are able to care for themselves.

Flights of Autumn

The migration from breeding lakes to wintering areas is spread out over a longer time and happens at a more leisurely pace than spring migration. Movements away from the breeding lakes may actually start to occur in July and August for pairs that failed at nesting. Other researchers and I have noticed a breakdown of nesting territories and absences of individuals or pairs in territories in which no chicks were hatched. We assume that these adults join groups of unmated and non-territorial adults that drift around from lake to lake during the summer season.

For loons with chicks, fall movements begin when the young are ten to twelve weeks old. Again, that can happen at a variety of times depending on the hatch date of the eggs. For a loon pair that initiated a nest in mid-May, the eggs would hatch in mid-June, and the chicks would be at flight stage by early September. For late nesters or those that nested a second or third time after early nest failures, the chicks may not hatch until after the Fourth of July. On my study area in Maine, we sometimes had chicks hatching in late July and even had a few in early August. Flight stage for these chicks could be as late as late October.

We don't know precisely how adults move to the coasts. Incidental observations of loons during the fall suggests that they move slowly stopping on large shallow lakes to feed. Loons have been reported in groups of several hundred on the Great Lakes and on large inland lakes throughout their range. Mille Lacs Lake in central Minnesota is perhaps the best known autumn stopping spot. Each year, hundreds, if not thousands, of loons can be seen during the middle of October on this large lake famous for its walleye fishing. When I lived in Maine, people would call me in the fall to report flocks of twenty to several hundred loons stopping on lakes such as Flagstaff Lake in western Maine and on the Belgrade Lakes in the central part of the state. Apparently, the loons are attracted to concentrations of fish that are near the surface in the fall.

Loons are reported on reservoirs in central states outside of their breeding range as autumn migration progresses. I clearly remember seeing a common loon on a reservoir in Oklahoma one fall. I had moved there from Maine to go to graduate school and was feeling a bit homesick for the fall colors of New England one weekend so I went to a nearby man-made lake to watch the ducks and other migratory birds. As I scanned the lake with my naked eye, I saw the unmistakable silhouette of a loon. My spirits improved immediately just by recognizing a creature I associated with the north country.

The young loons start their fall flight several weeks after the adults leave. Like the adults, they fly to nearby large lakes where they meet up with other young loons. They may stay on these lakes for weeks before finally heading south. It seems a bit odd that loons have not evolved so that loon chicks can find their way to the wintering grounds by flying with experienced adults the way that most waterfowl do. Instead, they are left to their own devices to get to the right places.

Because loons breed throughout Canada and Alaska, the fall migration covers many weeks and many miles. I have seen adult loons still passing through northern Wisconsin in late November. Presumably, these are birds from the far north of Canada. However, we know so little about the migration routes loons take that almost everything is speculation. Some loons may fly the shortest distance to the ocean and move to the south along the coast. There is some evidence that this may be the case. Reports of large numbers of loons along the north Atlantic and Pacific coasts are common in early winter.

Every year, some loons don't leave soon enough and are trapped by fast forming ice. When I was coordinating the LoonWatch program in Minnesota and Wisconsin in the late 1980s, I would get a few calls each year asking what I could do to help some loons that were about to be trapped. I never attempted what would be a dangerous rescue effort and counseled people about the laws of Nature and the survival of the fittest, but it never sounded quite as convincing as I hoped. None of us wanted to witness or even know that some loons were destined to swim in leads of open water that were closing in around them and that one night they would swim no more.

Autumn is a time when some of the greatest mortality occurs in loon populations. The rigors of the flight

may take their toll, but two other sources claim the lives of hundreds of loons. In some parts of the country, there are periodic outbreaks of a strain of botulism that affects waterbirds. The outbreaks occur in the same places every few years, keeping wildlife biologists on the lookout for dead and dying birds. One such place is Lake Michigan. Gulls, cormorants, loons, and other fish-eating birds ingest the toxin produced by a naturally occurring bacteria as they eat fish and drink the water. In high enough concentrations, the toxin causes muscle failure in the neck and the birds are unable to hold their heads out of the water. They die by drowning. The disease is aptly termed "limber neck disease" for the characteristic symptoms. There is no cure for the disease and no way to stop its outbreak or spread. Although it takes a toll on loons every few years, the numbers of loons that die are minuscule in relation to the total breeding population in North America.

One other odd and gruesome event may cut short a loon's flight to the ocean. On foggy and rainy nights, loons, which we believe migrate mostly during the day, sometimes mistake the ribbons of shiny, rain-soaked asphalt for rivers and attempt to land on them. They are injured as they land and most probably die within hours from getting hit by cars or from predators. They can't take off from land and will live only if people recognize what has happened and take them to nearby lakes or rivers. This occurrence is probably rare, but when it does happen, it makes the local news and word spreads quickly.

Most loons find their way to their winter homes where they begin a lifestyle that most of us would find rather un-loonlike based on our experience with them on their breeding lakes. But it is just part of the endless cycle for loons.

Winter

After watching loons all one's life on their breeding lakes, to see one on the ocean in the winter is a bit of a shock. Gone are the elegant breeding colors, replaced by a drab set of dark feathers on the head and back and light feathers on the chin and belly. Gone is the aggressive almost regal manner seen on nesting territories, given way to shy and almost reclusive behavior. Almost mute, they seem in their silence as if the sound has been turned off the television. Can these really be the same birds we watched and enjoyed all summer?

Common loons occupy a wide variety of winter habitats. Some winter inland on lakes, rivers, and reservoirs. Other hardy birds ride out winter swells on the Great Lakes. Most take up residence in coastal waters from

New Brunswick to northern Mexico on the Atlantic and Gulf coasts and from the tip of the Aleutian Islands to Baja California on the Pacific Coast. Some winter near shore and are readily visible from land. Others seek food far out to sea where they look for upwellings of nutrients (which attract fish) caused by the intersection of ocean currents.

Loons are counted and recorded in Christmas Bird Counts coordinated by the National Audubon Society and conducted by thousands of hardy volunteers. Large numbers are always seen along the Florida coast, around Cape Hatteras, and near Chincoteague, Virginia. Along with the Maine Audubon Society, I helped organize and participated in the first winter counts of loons along the entire coast of Maine in the early 1980s. Numbers that could be seen from land totaled only in the hundreds, but it let us know that there were a fair number of loons braving the sometimes fierce winter storms along Maine's rock-bound coast.

Loons go from aggressively territorial to loosely social during the short days of winter. It is common to see a small flock of loons feeding near shore in a bay during daylight hours and sleeping over the deepest part of the bay at night. They never become truly grouped, always keeping space between one another.

Loons feed on fish primarily, although at certain times and places they seem to either prefer or find more crabs and other crustaceans. Their habit of swallowing their meals before they come to the surface makes it difficult at best to determine their diets.

Until recently, we knew next to nothing about the loon's life in winter. A few researchers had recorded their daily and seasonal behavior, but it wasn't until Laurence Alexander started to delve into the mystery of large loon die-offs along the Florida and Georgia coasts that we started to see some of the complexity of winter loon ecology.

Die-offs of loons on the wintering grounds had been reported periodically, but a die-off of an estimated ten thousand or more loons in the early 1980s got everyone's attention. Frank Graham broke the news in "Mystery at Dog Island" in *Audubon* magazine. Despite the best efforts of wildlife pathologists, no clear cause for the mortality could be found. Laurence Alexander began a study to determine what was causing the deaths as well as how loons coped in their winter environs. In a tragic case of a life taken far too soon, he died of cancer before he could complete his work.

"Alexander," as he liked to be known, did discover a few things that have become the first pieces to the puzzle. Apparently, loons undergo a physiologically stressful period during their winter molt. They lose weight and

may become more susceptible to parasites, diseases, and pollutants they carry in their bodies. Those of us who knew Alexander and talked to him occasionally thought he was on to something big and important. His work lies much as he left it, incomplete and tempting in its speculations.

For now, our understanding of the loon's winter ecology is incomplete. Winter is the part of the endless cycle we understand the least and wonder about the most. It is a critical time for loons as they undergo great stress and prepare to come back to the northern lakes when the ice starts to disappear.

CHAPTER 5

Status and Distribution

Loons are birds of the Northern Hemisphere, rarely if ever wandering south of the equator. The common loon is primarily North American occurring also in Greenland and Iceland, and occasionally in Europe and Asia. The other four species occur around the globe in greater numbers.

In North America, Canada is heart of the common loon's breeding range. There are no good estimates from Canada, but some Canadian ornithologists have given educated guesses of a half million or more breeding pairs in their country. Outside of Alaska, common loons are not so common in

the continental United States. Minnesota leads the way. The so-called land of ten thousand lakes has twelve thousand or more adult loons during the summer.

It was no mean feat to develop a survey that would estimate the summer population of loons in Minnesota. Loons occur across the northern two thirds of that state, and many of the lakes are uninhabited by humans and just plain hard to get to. In 1989, the Minnesota Department of Natural Resources Nongame Wildlife Program and the Sigurd Olson Environmental Institute's LoonWatch project conducted the first ever statewide survey using over 800 volunteers. Lakes were selected in a fashion that would allow for statewide extrapolation of the data. Volunteers counted from shore and boats on lakes smaller than 500 acres while biologists counted loons from the air on a sample of large lakes. How well I remember photocopying maps of lakes, instructions, and data forms and answering hundreds of questions from interested volunteers. The volunteers came through as only avid loon lovers can and we were able to make our estimate of the largest population of common loons south of the Canadian border.

Wisconsin and Maine fall in behind Minnesota in numbers, each with several thousand. After those three states, everyone else's loon population is small. New York has close to a thousand.

Michigan, Montana, and New Hampshire have several hundred, while Vermont, North Dakota, Washington, Massachusetts, and Wyoming have fewer than a hundred each. Loons may be nesting in small numbers in Oregon, Pennsylvania, Illinois, Idaho, and Iowa. Nesting pairs are reported from these areas occasionally, but they are outliers in the breeding range.

Historical documents tell us that a hundred years or so ago common loons nested one full tier of states farther south than they do today. Nesting loons in Iowa, northern California, Illinois, and Pennsylvania were reasonably common. Over the last century, the breeding range has shrunk to the north, but the occasional records of nesters from these states suggests that loons may be reclaiming lost ground.

While the overall number of loons appears to be safe, the status of loons across the southern part of their breeding range has been a concern for the last several decades. Loons were on the verge of disappearing in states like New Hampshire, and populations in other states were on the decline. We didn't start getting accurate estimates of loons anywhere until the late 1970s. Most of that work occurred in New Hampshire where the situation seemed most dire and where the enthusiasm for protecting the remaining loons was strongest. It appears that loon populations bottomed out just about everywhere in

the lower 48 United States and in southern Ontario in the late 1970s. Since that time, most state populations have been recovering slowly. Some, like those in Vermont and Massachusetts seem stuck at very low numbers.

Today, the North American common loon population seems to have recovered the losses up to the 1970s. However, concern for future populations is still great as the insidious effects of pollution leave loons vulnerable and as the number of lakes being developed for summer homes and used for recreation increases almost exponentially.

The Taming of the Loon

The common loon was once thought to be exclusively a bird of the wilderness. Its reclusive nature and agitated response to the presence of people on its nesting lakes made us assume that loons couldn't tolerate the presence of humans. Early efforts to protect loons and preserve their habitat were focused on minimizing the effects of disturbance to loons on their nests and while they raised young. We even went so far as to say that loons should never be disturbed.

While we were correct to a degree, we had no idea that loons would demonstrate the flexibility in their behavior to adjust to fairly high levels of human use on the lakes they use for nesting. Today, we realize that if loons were indeed birds

of only the wilderness that there would be very few loons nesting in the lower 48 United States. Most loons share their lakes with either permanent or seasonal residents or recreationists who come for a fishing or camping trip.

Several studies were done in the early 1980s with the intent of determining just how loons were affected by human use of nesting lakes. To the best of my knowledge, the researchers had no idea the other folks were doing similar studies. The three studies were about as spread out as they could get— one was in the Alaska, another in Minnesota, and the third in Maine. They all reported the same surprising results. What wasn't surprising was that loons were affected by human use of the lakes. Compared to loons nesting on lakes without human use, they either had lower nest success or were able to raise fewer young. The surprising part was that loons on lakes with human residents and recreational use showed behavioral adaptations that allowed them to somewhat compensate for the disturbance and to nest and raise young at rates not all that much lower than loons on the wild lakes. The loons on the wild lakes actually showed greater behavioral distress when people were around than the loons on the developed lakes. It appeared that loons were able to tolerate people after all.

We really shouldn't be too shocked by this. Many animals have been able to adapt to the presence of people. In fact, a number of species are doing much better today in a culturally modified landscape than they ever did before the country was so settled. Think about the eastern phoebes, barn swallows, and cliff swallows who nest over your porch light or under the eaves of your house. White-tailed deer are thriving in urban parks and suburban areas. Coyotes are sometimes seen roaming the streets of Los Angeles. I've seen a number of bald eagle nests near campgrounds, along roads, and within a stone's throw of people's houses.

We never gave the loon a chance. Before we got to know loons well, we assumed that they had rigid behavior patterns and that they would be unable to change. It went along with the stereotype of loons being primitive birds, relics just barely surviving in the modern world.

Most people who live on a lake with a pair of loons know that the loons have simply accepted boats, canoes, lakeshore houses, and all of the sounds of human habitation as part of their environment. Yes, they have their limits, and when the lake becomes too crowded, too noisy, and the nest or chicks are disturbed too many times, the loons pull up stakes and go away. However, if they are given enough space and privacy, loons sometimes do very well on lakes with people. They may even occasionally enjoy greater nest success and raise more young because they are on a lake with people. On these lakes there may be fewer predators and a group of people who watch over the family protectively. On the other hand, some lakes have increased populations of raccoons, skunks, crows, and gulls, and these predators are just too much for the loons to fend off.

I have always characterized loons as curiously wary. They want to know what is happening on a lake and will investigate almost anything. At the same time, they are wary and will disappear at the first sign of danger. As they have had more frequent encounters with people, their curiosity has provided some memorable experiences.

Many of us have had close encounters with loons who have become used to us being around. Sometimes, these have been a surprise to both the loon and the person. Many people have told me of an experience I have had several times myself. They are out fishing or canoeing and out of the blue a loon pops up right next to their boat. The loon either calls immediately and dives or it looks surprised and checks out the people and their craft. More than once, I have been paddling a canoe, seen a loon swim underneath the canoe, and watched the loon come up just a few feet away.

A man who was staying on a wild lake in northern Maine with just two old cabins on it that were rarely used by people told me that he listened to opera on his portable radio every evening while he was renting one of the cabins. And every night, a loon that he presumed was the same one, would swim right up to the shore where he was sitting in his lawn chair. The loon would swim back and forth in front of the man apparently trying to determine the source of the sound. The loon got so close he told me that he could literally count the stripes in its necklace and the spots on its back.

I have heard stories and seen pictures of loons that have become so tame that they will follow a fishing boat looking for a handout of live bait or they will come to a dock doing the same. A few loons have become so tame that they will even crawl up on land and let people approach them. Some loons on high recreational use lakes in New Hampshire have become so used to people that they will not leave their nests even when a boat or canoe approaches. We call these loons "stickers" as opposed to "flushers," which are the loons that leave their nest and take to the water immediately upon seeing a boat. Judy McIntyre has told me of putting her hand under a loon on a nest to lift it slightly so that she could see the eggs.

"Sticking" to a nest instead of flushing from it is one of the behavioral changes that has allowed loons on developed lakes to sometimes have equal or higher rates of nest success and chick rearing than loons on wild lakes. Researchers have actually measured the distance to which an incubating loon will allow a boat to approach before leaving the nest. Although individual loons show great variation, the general pattern is clear. Loons that nest on developed lakes allow boats to get much closer than those on undeveloped lakes.

The loons that exhibit extreme modifications of their behavior are the exception and I hope it stays that way. While I am glad that loons have been able to adjust to our presence, I want them to maintain an element of wildness, a certain aloofness, and with it a sense of dignity even if we are the ones who attribute that characteristic to them. It seems better to share a lake with a bird that is still wild and has its limits. It makes us appreciate them more and forces us to adjust our behavior so that we are able to coexist with them.

The Acid Test

Changes in the aquatic environments have always created challenges for the adaptive powers of loons. In the long term, evolution has wrought modifications of the loon's physical and chemical make-up. Changes over shorter periods of time require flexibility in behavior. For the most part, loons have been able to adjust to the presence of

people by altering their behavior. However, the changes people bring to the loon's habitat are happening at a far greater rate than what probably occurred before people occupied North America. These changes represent the ultimate challenge for loons.

Perhaps no more insidious threat to loons exists than the changes that occur in lakes as they become acidified and polluted in other ways. Loons are restricted to lakes within their breeding range and do not have the option of occupying other habitats. They must make the best of what a lake offers them.

The concern that arose over acid rain and other kinds of acid deposition in the mid-1970s was not lost on conservationists concerned about loons. It seemed obvious that lakes that lost their fish would soon lose their loons. Research conducted in the 1980s demonstrated that the picture was not nearly that simple. Lake acidification and the reactions of loons to it covered a wide spectrum of possibilities.

There have been two important studies of the effects of lake acidification on loons. One was done by Robert Alvo near the Sudbury region of Ontario and the other by Karl Parker in the Adirondack Park of upstate New York. The studies were similar in their attempt to discover if differences existed in loons' abilities to raise young successfully on lakes of different acidities. They were different in that the lakes on Rob's study area were far more acidic and had been so longer than those on Karl's study area. Together, the studies provide a good picture of how acidification affects loons and how loons react to changes in their habitat.

Rob Alvo (then at Ontario's Trent University) found that loons would return to fishless lakes year after year even if they were unable to raise young successfully. On the most acidic lakes, the adult loons would nest and hatch young while finding food for themselves on nearby lakes. They fed their chicks small aquatic insects and algae while continuing to find food for themselves elsewhere. The chicks grew slowly, became listless, and eventually died. On the less acidic lakes, the adults were able to find enough food for the young on the breeding lake and more loon chicks survived to the flight stage.

On the lakes he studied, Karl Parker from Syracuse University found that loons on acidified lakes could find enough food to raise their young to flight stage even on some fishless lakes. Instead of feeding their chicks fish, they provided dragonfly larvae and other insect food. It is possible that the lakes in his study area had more and a wider variety of insects and that they were less polluted with aluminum and other heavy metals that are present near Sudbury.

Karl noticed that adult loons actually could catch food more often on lakes with fewer fish, but that the increased success rate was offset by the small size of the prey items. Thus, the loons could catch food more easily, but had to catch even more to feed the chicks enough. On some lakes, the only fish that could be caught regularly were yellow perch of a size that was almost too large for the chicks to swallow.

The adults didn't seem to have a problem feeding the chicks while they were very small. However, as the chicks grew, their food demands increased at an exponential rate, and it may have been difficult to find enough food when the chicks were growing most rapidly and using some of their energy to molt feathers. As Gary Dulin found in his studies of sibling rivalry, it is hard enough for adult loons to raise two young because of sibling rivalry and the dominant chick's first dibs at food. It seems likely that on acidified lakes the rivalry is even more intense although no one has studied this carefully.

One of the most intriguing findings of Karl Parker's study was his observations of adult loons flying with fish in their bills. He saw this only three times, but the adults appeared to be ferrying fish from a nearby lake back to the lake on which they nested and were raising young. Karl speculated that they might be bringing back the fish for the chicks as red-throated, Arctic, and Pacific loons are known to do commonly. These were the first and the only documented observations to date of this behavior in common loons, and so, it is obviously not widespread. However, it again points out the range of possible behaviors in loons and their ability to respond to changing environmental conditions. Perhaps this is how other behavioral changes come about, one loon at a time responding to new challenges.

Although Parker's and Alvo's studies could not demonstrate conclusively that lake acidification was negatively affecting loons, they pointed out that territorial affinity will cause loons to come back to the same lakes to nest and attempt to raise young even if there is not enough food in the lake. Apparently, over the millions of years of loon evolution, it has never been important for loons to discriminate for the presence of food. If the lake had clear enough water to see through, it probably had fish and other kinds of food. Now, however, the clarity of a lake, which increases with acidification, may not be a good cue for loons to use.

The loon's ability to adapt to change probably masks the deleterious effects of lake acidification. Certainly, over time, lakes that lose their fish will not be able to support loons or other species that rely on the productivity of the lake. Loons and other species may hang on for a time, raising a few young now and then, but we have no idea if loon populations will be able to sustain

themselves. Only time will tell.

As if acidification weren't enough, loons face another serious problem. Over the past ten years, scientists have been finding elevated amounts of mercury in the tissues of fish and in loons and other fish-eating birds and mammals. Mercury contamination is so high in some parts of the country that fish consumption advisories for people are issued. At highest risk are pregnant women and small children. Large predatory fish, such as walleye and northern pike, are the species of fish with the highest concentration of mercury. Neither of these species appear to be primary sources of food for loons, and loons are limited to fish that can be swallowed all at once. Nonetheless, the amount of fish consumed by loons over the course of the summer puts loons at high risk in some areas.

Jack Barr studied loons living in a lake and river system in Ontario that was known to have high levels of mercury in its organic form called methyl mercury. The organic form of mercury is the one that enters food chains. Like some other kinds of chemicals, methyl mercury accumulates as it is passed up through the food chain. A small aquatic insect may have only one part of mercury per billion in its body. The larger aquatic insects that eat it may have one part per one hundred million. The small fish eating the large insects may have one part per ten million. The medium-sized fish eating the small fish may have one part per million. And the loon eating the medium-sized fish may accumulate mercury at a concentration of several parts per million, which is high enough to cause problems.

Jack found that loons with two to three parts per million of methyl mercury in their brain tissues nested less frequently than normal, showed poor attentiveness to their nests, and had less territorial drive than would be expected from normal loons. Adult male loons had higher concentrations of mercury than females and the males were often emaciated. It appeared that mercury poisoning may have affected the males' abilities to fish effectively. Not being able to fish is not the only problem. Because male loons share incubation duties with the females and also spend time defending the territory, any decrease in the male's incentive to do either of these important tasks will likely affect the pair's ability to successfully raise young.

Mercury is also passed from female loons to their young during the egg laying process. Thus, young loons with parents that already have a lot of mercury in their bodies start out life with two strikes against them.

Mercury is not found only in lakes and rivers near sources of industrial pollution. Studies conducted by the Minnesota Pollution Control Agency found high levels of mercury in loons in both northeastern and northwestern Minnesota, far from the nearest sources of mercury. In Wisconsin, many lakes have fish with high mercury levels, and there is reason to think the loons in these lakes have high levels of mercury as well. Mike Meyer, a Wisconsin Department of Natural Resources Researcher, has started a long-term study of the effects of mercury on large numbers of loons to determine what effect mercury might have on the overall numbers of loons in an area over time. His preliminary findings suggest that on lakes with high acidity and correspondingly high levels of mercury in fish and loons, fewer young loons are raised than on similar lakes with lower acidity and mercury. In Wisconsin and Minnesota, the levels of mercury found in loons is already higher than those found by Jack Barr. Perhaps these two large centers of loon population are not as secure as their sizes would suggest.

There is a scary link between mercury and lake acidification. It appears that as lakes become more acidic, the bacteria responsible in part for converting inorganic mercury to its dangerous organic form increases. So, as lakes become acidic, they may also liberate more mercury into the food web. Fewer fish in acidic lakes means that each fish may have high mercury levels, and the chance that a fish eaten by a loon will have lots of mercury is high.

We do not know the sources for the mercury found in loons. Some of it is certainly from the natural sources of mercury in lakes. It is likely that some of it comes from industrial pollutants which may travel hundreds of miles as airborne particles. Mercury is certainly present in fish on the loons' breeding lakes. It may also be in fish eaten on the wintering grounds. The dead loons Laurence Alexander and others found off the coasts of Florida and Georgia had high levels of mercury, but we don't know where it originated.

While not as serious and widespread a threat as lake acidification and mercury poisoning, fluctuations in lake levels caused by dams used for hydroelectric power generation are a problem for loons, particularly in the northeastern part of the United States and Canada. If dramatic fluctuations occur while loons are on their nests, the nests can be flooded or left high and dry. Loons have surprised us in their ability to deal with these changes. As water levels rise, some loons are able to build up their nests. Lowering water levels may leave a nest over a hundred feet from water, but many loons will plod slowly from water to the nest to continue incubation. Obviously, these nests are more subject to desertion by the adults and to predation. While loons have again demonstrated their behavioral flexibility in dealing with lake levels, they have their limits. For example, water levels rising over a foot will wipe

out most of the loon nests because they can't build up their nests that much. Similarly, a drop of more than a foot and a half will cause most loons to abandon their nests.

Lead poisoning is a problem of unknown proportions. Loons and other water birds occasionally ingest lead sinkers lost by fishermen. The lead is ground up in the gizzard and can be lethal in very small amounts. There is no accurate estimate of the numbers of loons that die from lead poisoning, but enough are discovered to cause us to think that it may be a significant problem in some areas. Three separate studies of loon carcasses found lead poisoning as the cause of death: (1) 6 percent

from 18 states, including wintering areas; (2) 53 percent in loons on freshwater lakes in New England; and (3) 39 percent from freshwater lakes in Michigan.

There may even be a link between lead poisoning and mercury. Loons with lead poisoning often have high levels of mercury in their bodies, suggesting that the mercury causes abnormal behavior and an increased intake of lead sinkers.

Less frequently observed is the problem of fishing hooks and lines and commercial fishing nets. Reports of loons drowned in fishing nets in Canada and in the Great Lakes have always bothered conservationists. While some of these loons have provided information about the food habits of loons, the losses are disturbing. We don't know how many loons die in nets, but the number is easily in the thousands on an annual basis. Some work has been done to look for net designs that will allow loons to escape without reducing the effectiveness on fish capture, but it is in its infancy. For now, as long as there are nets in the water, loons as well as fish will be caught.

Occasionally, we hear reports of loons, particularly nearly grown loon chicks, swallowing a minnow on the end of a fishing hook or even a lure. Unattended lines seem to be the worst culprits. The loons become entangled in fishing lines and have to be rescued. Often, all that can be done is to remove the line around the loon's body. If the hook has been swallowed, the line is cut as close to the hook as possible and we hope for the best.

The modern world has created many new problems for loons. They adjust and adjust, stretching their behavior to its limits. When those limits are reached, we can only expect that future populations of loons will be smaller, less widely distributed, and in greater danger of long-term losses.

Loon Rangers to the Rescue

While there seem to be too many problems to hold out hope for the loon's future, there are some silver linings to the gloomy clouds. We know that loon populations have been recovering since the 1970s and that individual loons have showed an amazing ability to cope with some of the problems. Perhaps the most exciting and stirring story, however, is that of people who have become so enchanted with loons that they have begun to make the loons' lives better.

I fondly refer to these people as "loon rangers." I didn't coin the term, but I like it. And I'd like to think that I'm a loon ranger, too.

Perhaps you are a loon ranger or know someone who is. They aren't always easy to spot, but many of them leave no doubt. You know the type. They wear tee shirts with images of loons on the front. Their car sports a bumper sticker that says, "Love a Loon." But most importantly, they *do* things. On the weekends, they volunteer their time to help conduct a loon survey in their area. They present educational programs at local schools. They put up signs at boat ramps that alert boaters to the presence of loon families. And they care, sometimes so much that they live and die emotionally with the ups and downs of the loon family on their lakes.

Some loon rangers belong to organizations that promote the protection and conservation of loons. One such organization, New Hampshire Audubon's Loon Preservation Committee, has long been recognized as a leader in this effort. Its goal is to help New Hampshire's loon population recover to a level where it can be taken off the state's threatened species list. Another, the Sigurd Olson Environmental Institute's LoonWatch program, conducts public education programs and population surveys and supports research efforts in Minnesota and Wisconsin where loon populations are large and appear to be in no imminent danger. LoonWatch takes the philosophy that an ounce of prevention now will prevent a pound of cure needed later. The North American Loon Fund promotes loon conservation on a continental scale. It supports loon research through financial grants, is a clearinghouse for information about loons, and gathers loon researchers and others together periodically to update the status of knowledge of common loons.

Loon rangers do a wide variety of things. Some band together in lake patrols to keep boaters from approaching loon nests or young chicks too closely during busy recreational weekends. They pass out informational materials about loons to summer visitors who may visit a loon lake for only a week or two. Many participate in loon festivals put on by their local loon protection organization. Loon rangers with a knack for public speaking present educational programs about loons to schoolchildren and to adult groups.

One activity that has captured the imagination of many is the construction of artificial nest islands. In the 1970s, Judy McIntyre pioneered the use of small floating islands to aid in her study of loons in Minnesota. The islands are constructed of cedar logs fashioned into a square about three or four feet on a side. Wire mesh is fastened to the logs and sod and vegetation placed on top of the mesh. Sometimes, flotation materials are placed underneath the mesh to prevent the island from becoming water-logged and sinking. Canopies are placed on some to decrease predation on the eggs by gulls and crows.

The islands were first used to provide loons better nesting sites in New Hampshire. There, many of the nests were being destroyed by predators like skunks and raccoons. Also, the fluctuating water levels on lakes with hydroelectric dams were flooding nests or leaving them high and dry. The islands gave loons a safer location to place their nests because they adjusted to changes in lake levels. Years of monitoring the islands showed that success in hatching young increased. It is believed that the use of artificial islands, or rafts as they are also known, helped speed up the recovery of New Hampshire's loon population.

Artificial islands are now in use in most states from Maine to Minnesota to Washington. They are not a panacea for loon problems, however, and do not belong on every lake. Organizations like LoonWatch stress that they should be used only when other natural nest sites are not available, when water-level fluctuations cause problems, or when mainland nests are subjected to repeated predation.

Like all artificial solutions, rafts need to be maintained by people. Natural solutions seem more desirable because they don't require the constant input of people. The artificial islands need to be taken out and dried in the fall, put back in the lake right after ice-out, and repaired periodically. They have proven their worth in many situations, but we don't want loons to have to rely on them for the majority of their nests sites.

This disappoints many people who would like to have a nesting island right in front of *their* cottage. Unlike bluebird houses or wood duck nest boxes, however, loon nesting islands need to be placed in just the right spot in the lake.

I was once told that loons were a fad, that their popularity with people would lessen in the matter of a few years. Loon paraphernalia would sit on the stockroom shelves and the birds themselves would cease to be the focus of our research and conservation efforts and of our enjoyment. That twenty-year-old prophecy may yet come true, but the loon rangers who come to the loons' rescue every year make me think not.

EPILOGUE

When I began writing this book, it brought back many old pleasant memories of interactions I have had with loons and with the people who study and watch them. I thought of the wonderful success story of recovering loon populations across the continent. In general, I was upbeat.

As I put the finishing touches to the manuscript, however, I am troubled. Despite our best efforts, it appears that loons are losing ground to the unseen but powerful forces of pollution. Many loons have mercury loads so high that they should glow in the dark. Lead poisoning afflicts many more loons than should pick up lead sinkers by chance.

Loon populations have been rebounding since the mid-1970s, increasing their numbers and range. Their ability to modify their behavior to the rapidly changing world is nothing short of astounding. Surely, none but the most optimistic of us studying loons in the 1980s would have expected loons to adapt so rapidly and so greatly.

Now, I sense a turning of the tide. How can loons and other creatures adapt to the very poisoning of their flesh?

Clearly, the time has come to face the music. If no more mercury, no more lead, and no more sulfur dioxide are released into the environment, there may be a chance to weather yet another great decline in loon populations until these contaminants are flushed from aquatic ecosystems and they become healthy places to live again. If, however, we continue to pump these contaminants into the air, soil, and water, loons and other creatures are in trouble.

And who are we to think that none of this is affecting us? We, too, are at the top of many food webs, no different from the loon.

I do not relish the thought of leaving you with such gloomy thoughts, but any book that celebrates loons must also recognize the dark forces that threaten them. Enjoy the loons, dear reader. Learn more about them. Seek the spiritual experiences that create awe and wonder. But save some of your energy for the battles that must be won if our sons and daughters and theirs in turn will have the same opportunities afforded to us.

Selected Reading List

Much has been written about loons in the last decade in both the popular and scientific literature.

Tom Klein wrote and published the first major popular book on loons, *Loon Magic* (NorthWord Press, Inc.). It still stands as one of the most complete narratives as well as having dozens of the best photographs. Its children's form, *Loon Magic for Kids*, is great for young loon lovers.

Judith McIntyre wrote the definitive scientific work of the time in 1988. *The Common Loon: Spirit of Northern Lakes* (University of Minnesota Press) is a readable account of Judy's own field studies.

The most literary book about loons yet to appear is Joan Dunning's *The Loon: Voice of the Wilderness* (Yaokee Publishing). Not only did Joan write eloquently about loons, she also illustrated the book with wonderful line drawings and watercolors.

Kate Crowley and Mike Link's 1987 book, *Love of Loons* (Voyageur Press) is another early loon book. Kate and Mike added a strong human element to the story of loons. Their book contains numerous anecdotes of loons' interactions with people.

The most recent offering about loons is Terry McEneaney's *The Uncommon Loon* (Northland Publishing). Unlike other loon books, it focuses only on the common loon and gives a western perspective based on Terry's experiences as a wildlife ecologist in Yellowstone National Park.

Technical writings about loons appear in a variety of scientific journals, reports from state wildlife agencies and loon conservation organizations, and in Master's theses and doctoral dissertations. These can be difficult to find, but two excellent sources are the North American Loon Fund, 6 Lily Pond Road, Gilford, New Hampshire 03246, and the LoonWatch Program, Sigurd Olson Environmental Institute, Northland College, Ashland, Wisconsin 54806.